TALES FROM

Heart *of the* Country

The Midlands offer some of the most varied landscapes in the UK. From the dramatic
Malvern Hills which interrupt the surrounding plateau like a giant sleeping policeman . . .

TALES FROM
Heart *of the* Country

TONY FRANCIS

Edited by
Wendy Dickinson

Kingfisher
TELEVISION PRODUCTIONS LIMITED

First published in 2002 by Kingfisher Television Productions,
Carlton Studios, Lenton Lane, Nottingham NG7 2NA

ISBN 0-9540578-1-3

Supported by The East Midlands Media Initiative -
part funded by the European Regional Development Fund.

A CIP catalogue record for this book is available from the British Library.

Front cover photograph: Alan Olley
Design and production by Charlie Webster
Printed in Great Britain by the Bath Press.

This book accompanies the television series Heart of the Country
© Carlton Television Limited, made by Kingfisher Television Productions.
Series producer: Tony Francis
Executive producer: Duncan Rycroft

...to the flatlands of Lincolnshireshire where the sunrises and sunsets are every bit as magical as the favourite crop.

Contents

A sign of global warming? Daffodils were out at Chatsworth by the end of February. Bluebells were early everywhere too.

Acknowledgements

I would like to thank everyone whose inspiration and support have made this book possible, particularly those who have featured in Heart of the Country over the years and the viewers who keep wanting more.

I'm also indebted to the individuals and organisations that have helped us to illustrate the book – including viewers, amateur and professional photographers, local newspapers and local authorities. They include:

Gloucestershire County Council; West Oxfordshire Tourism; South Warwickshire Tourism; High Peak Borough Council; Lincolnshire County Council; Derbyshire Dales District Council; Herefordshire Tourism; Worcestershire Tourism; Leicestershire County Council; Melton Borough Council; The Great Central Railway; Stoke Sentinel; Shropshire Star; Shrewsbury Chronicle; Leicester Mercury; Bucks & Winslow Advertiser; Daventry Express; Imogen Skirving; Pauline Hannigan; James Waddell; Marc & Tia Swan, Crooked House, PO Box 13, Knighton Do LD8 2WE, Chris Chapman; David Rayner; Robert Dean; Scarthin Bookshop; Youlgreave Water Works; George Rezseter; Eckford Sweet Pea Society; Andrew Fox; British Horological Institute, Viscount Middleton; The Laurie Lee Collection; Gary Moyes; Laura Dickinson; Alan Marshall; Ken & Jen Mellor, Geoff Hallam; The Heights of Abraham; David Spencer, Graham Pearce, Lionel Heap; John Taylor; Paula Clair; Ann Blanchard; Peter Tree www.petertree.co.uk, Saffron Tree; Mike Williams; Christine Everard, Robin Grant.

Funny how times change. My home county, Leicestershire, is now populated by London commuters. It's quicker to get to the capital from here than from parts of Greater London.

Introduction

In 14 years of producing Heart of the Country, the question I've been asked more than any other is "How do you find all your stories?" The short answer is by keeping our eyes open and asking questions.

Who could possibly live in a dilapidated house like that? Why is that farmer growing sunflowers? How come that brook has appeared out of nowhere? Why does that church tower have a violin for a weathervane?

It's usually when filming one story that we come across another. You'd be surprised how often someone in a pub somewhere will say something like: "By the way, did you hear about the nude farmer?" And off we go again.

The fruits of these encounters and conversations are gathered for the first time in print, which answers the second most popular question: "When are you going to bring out a book?" This is the first of what we hope will be a collection of books with the Heart of the Country stamp. The theme is curious tales – from the chap who dug his own grave, to the run away Labrador that lived in the wild for seven years and defied all attempts to capture it. You couldn't invent stories like that. Enjoy reading them and rest assured that there are plenty more where they came from. If you don't believe me, just keep watching Heart of the Country.

Tony

In The Beginning...

Until you get to know it, the Vale of Belvoir can be a disconcerting place. It sounds more appealing than it is. At first glance, monotonously flat and featureless, within easy striking distance of Nottingham, Grantham and Melton Mowbray but the sort of place you don't go to. At least, I never had, despite growing up in Leicester. We thought it was inhabited by people in smocks and flowerpot hats who worried sheep.

I changed my tune years later, in the very early days of Heart of the Country, when we set up office in a hamlet called Barnstone next to the Blue Circle Cement Works. Tasteful eh? It wasn't by choice – just that there was a television facilities company already there. We liked the way they worked and decided to take up their offer of sharing the rent of what amounted to little more than a portakabin. That's where Heart of the Country began 13 years ago and that was my introduction to a different pace of life. I'm now a Vale of Belvoir convert. Let me tell you how it came about.

None of the bedrooms had a key. So what? The chef was having a nervous breakdown while 20 guests waited to be served. C'est la vie.

To begin with, I had to find somewhere to stay overnight when I was assembling the programmes at Barnstone, a two and a half hour drive from home. Fortunately our new secretary, Jayne Stubbs, was a native and gave me the first of many priceless pieces of advice. She recommended Langar Hall in the next village but failed to warn me about Imogen Skirving, the diminutive character who owned it. If I thought Fawlty Towers existed only in John Cleese's imagination, I was about to be disabused.

It wasn't so much the lack of a bedroom key that caught me off guard, as the appearance of a complete stranger beside my dressing table in the middle of the night. The ghost of Langar Hall? Not exactly – just an errant guest who'd had one too many brandies and forgotten his room number. Quite a baptism. The Holiday Inn it wasn't. You don't get the hotel proprietor sharing breakfast with you at the Holiday Inn, much less apologising for 'that little hiccup last night.'

I left for a day's editing without having a chance to look around Langar Hall but it had certainly made an impression. I was looking forward to a return visit, intrigued that such an off-the-wall establishment could exist in the middle of nowhere. How on earth did Imogen attract enough customers to make Langar Hall a profitable business?

When I returned and saw it by daylight I understood. A slightly run-down late Georgian family home with pale-orange rendering which looked delightful in the sunshine but, on closer inspection, was starting to flake off. Langar Hall is practically joined to the parish church in the only undulating countryside for miles around. Peculiar that. There was steep descent to the lake where the view over the 'ha ha' to the sheep meadow and Cropwell Bishop beyond, gave the brief illusion of standing on a Cotswold escarpment.

However, the reason most customers sought out Langar Hall rather than checking into the Novotel or the Post House in Nottingham could be summed up in two words. Imogen Skirving. All of five foot in her stockinged feet but tightly packed. On the many occasions I've stayed there, I've never seen her down in the dumps. Distracted, occasionally, by troublesome chefs or staff who'd gone AWOL, but never down.

Langar Hall was the family home, owned by her father, Geoffrey Huskinson, a star sportsman of his day. Geoffrey was a real all-rounder, playing cricket for Nottinghamshire, rugger for England and tennis at Wimbledon. Imogen recalls many of the great names of cricket – including Don Bradman – staying as house guests in her youth. But it was guests of a different kind she welcomed after her father's death, opening as a B & B in 1984 and then as a fully-fledged hotel. It was the only way she could afford to stay in the house. In the early days she ran it, for the most part on her own, assisted only now and again by a somewhat moody daughter. At times she was so broke she couldn't afford a car and would roar around the countryside on a motorbike collecting provisions.

Imogen's USP (unique selling point) was her scatty nonchalance about the hotel business and about life itself. Oh, she cared fervently about people and their foibles and she loved every day that she woke up, but I always had the impression that none of it should be taken too seriously. So what if none of the bedrooms had a key? The chef was having a nervous breakdown while 20 guests were waiting for dinner? C'est la vie!

Everyone in the Vale of Belvoir knows Imogen Skirving. The pocket dynamo has friends in high places and most of them make a beeline for Langar Hall, given half a chance.

One day when I arrived she dashed out of the house, tripping over two Pekinese which fussed around her ankles, and asked to be excused for an hour. She was just popping to Jessops department store in Nottingham to replace two mallets from the croquet set. The chef and sous-chef had been using them as steak tenderisers before falling out. There followed a pitched duel during which the steak flew ceiling-wards and the mallets lost their heads. It wasn't so terminal that the chateaubriand had to be struck off the menu in favour of reindeer, but the diners would be inconsolable if they couldn't enjoy a game of croquet after their port and Stilton.

Which brings me to the nosh. Outstanding. The soups were all home-made, so was the bread. The entrees changed nightly as sea bass, venison, mullet, rabbit, beef, pork and home-reared lamb chased each other's tails for prominence. And the Stilton! We were only two miles from the world's greatest dairy at Colston Bassett so it was necessarily top drawer. Big fat wheels of blue-veined cheese from which Imogen excavated generous dollops with a spoon. This, apparently, was the way one should eat it.

Dinner, or supper, was usually designed as a communal affair. Unless you were a leper or in the throes of a heavy attack of halitosis, you had to have a pretty good excuse not to join in. That meant dining in the company of perfect strangers whose self-consciousness was demolished by the common bond we shared — we'd all elected to stay at this benign 'asylum' where the owner was quite likely to burst into an operatic aria while pouring out the wine. It would happen without

warning. An explosion of Verdi in a piercing vibrato. The first time I witnessed it I almost choked on a caper. The second time I was tempted to join in but thought better of it in the interests of fraternal harmony. She had a good voice, did Imogen, and not an ounce of inhibition. What prompted her to metamorphose from dining room queen to Diva is anyone's guess. I sometimes wondered if it wasn't a side effect of the Dr Bach's remedies she kept about her person to counteract every emotional swing.

It didn't take me long to realise that Langar Hall wasn't simply a good place to stay, it was a documentary – or at least a study in rural eccentricity. Imogen might as well have torn up the hotel management template. As loveable and scatterbrained as her methods were though, she wasn't especially proud of her accounting system. Instead of dividing her day's takings into designated bank accounts, it all went into the same pot. Well, to be precise, an antique china hen. To be fair, she had more than one. There were several, placed strategically around the Hall. A guest would pay and she would stick the money in the nearest hen. If she had only remembered how much she'd put in – or even which hen she'd used – things might have been different, but money was either forgotten or seemed to disappear, and her laissez-faire attitude meant that people took advantage.

Imogen did employ the occasional waiter who scampered off with the cutlery or was caught helping himself to a crate of Burgundy in the cellar. She confided to me one day that anarchy would have to cease and forward planning would have to be introduced if Langar Hall was to fulfil its potential. That said, she

Little did I realise that behind the ochre exterior of this dreamy location lurked an extraordinary hotel-keeper with the quirkiness of Basil Fawlty but twice the charm. Her name was Imogen.

pottered off to a self-improvement course at the Novotel. When she returned the hens were banished, a financial manager was appointed and a set of keys cut for the bedrooms. I'm happy to say that Imogen was then able to resume her off-the-wall style of hotel-keeping, confident that the basics were in place.

Back to music for a moment. Langar Hall's musical evenings were the stuff of legend — still are, although Crispin must have been difficult to replace. The roly-

poly supply teacher-cumwine waiter-cum-entertainer was indeed several people squashed into one. A better off-the-cuff pianist and songwriter would be difficult to find. And his impersonation of Laurel and Hardy to his own accompaniment was quite brilliant. He WAS Oliver Hardy. Why he didn't go on to become a star I shall never know.

I make no apology for confessing that we've filmed at Langar Hall on many occasions over the years. I recall a particularly funny day shortly after Imogen was granted a licence to hold weddings and wedding receptions. It was too good an opportunity to miss. The happy couple were happy to be filmed and May did us proud with a breathtakingly beautiful day. The hawthorn was in fragrant blossom and cow parsley fringed the croquet lawn with its lace-like whiteness.

You can keep your Skibo Castle — at that moment, I couldn't think of a finer place to get married. The only fly in the ointment was the arrival of a sewage truck to empty the septic tank. Burly men in boiler suits leaped from the wagon, brandishing hosereels as though they'd been invited to the reception. It's the only time I've seen Imogen blanche. Needless to say, we talked amongst ourselves and did our utmost to stay indoors for the next 20 minutes while the consequence of Langar's magnificent suppers was sucked into a disposal vehicle with a deafening roar and an indescribable stench. Of all the days to choose!

I can heartily recommend Langar Hall. It has lost none of its magic, nor capacity to surprise. Furthermore, the moody daughter discovered transcendental meditation after running away to the foothills of the Himalayas and marrying an Indian Yoga teacher. I dare say a dose of that from time to time would benefit Imogen. Her belief in alternative medicine is already fairly solid, though it did take some time for her to get to understand her new son-in-law. Despite being one of the most accomplished hostesses in the country, she found it hard to make conversation with someone who spends most of his time upside down.

The Village That Broke In Half

The village of Jackfield is more or less invisible. Look in most road atlases and it just doesn't exist. Not a mention. Perhaps the AA and the RAC assumed that the famous 1950's landslip had wiped it off the face of the earth. They were nearly right. However, reports of Jackfield's demise have been grossly exaggerated. It still clings, in a dare-devilish way, to each bank of the river Severn, north of Ironbridge. Bent, cracked and buckled it may be; erased it certainly isn't.

They called it 'the fag end of the world' in the 1800's, when smoke belched from Jackfield's chimneys. The air was as thick as gravy; the sun did not linger. It was a fully-employed village of the Industrial Revolution. One thousand, five hundred people beavering away as though their lives depended on it, which of

The Severn Trow in its heydey around the 1900's. The factory behind is on the far bank of the river.

course they did. Smoke, grime, drink and crime stirred into one effervescent cocktail. I've seen the photographs and they're not pretty...

At the centre of it all was the Jackfield Encaustic and Decorative Tile Works. That proud name is still emblazoned along the side of the factory, where 700 men fired the clay that turned this once-lovely corner of Shropshire into the centre of the British tile making industry.

They were wild, raucous days, when beer-swilling trow men hauled their flat-bottomed boats up and down the Ironbridge Gorge. River ports like Jackfield bristled with whorehouses. Sailors who never saw the sea sampled everything else a seaport could offer. At its height the village boasted no fewer than 30 brothels. Some are still there, converted into pubs or houses.

The village cracked and crumbled as though it had been hit by a meteorite before sliding slowly into the river. Jackfield's industrial revolution was over in 24 hours.

But the high life couldn't last forever. Nature – provoked and plundered by industrial man for 150 years – finally struck back. Carelessly, they'd stopped pumping water out of the ancient clay mines. The effect was calamitous. In April, 1952 the village cracked and crumbled as though it had been hit by a meteorite and slithered into the river. Houses split in two; roads disappeared. The railway line – a major umbilical cord – was twisted into knots like a piece of wire. Jackfield's industrial revolution was over in 24 hours. The village ceased to exist.

No wonder it isn't on the map. You just have to believe it's there and point your car in the general direction. It's well worth the effort because Jackfield does exist. Okay, the population has shrunk to a handful and they don't make tiles anymore, but there is a strikingly ornate Victorian church made entirely from local bricks and tiles and the remains of Mrs Dirk's tin sweetshop which produced original humbugs. You'll need decent suspension on your vehicle because the main artery is the track of the old Severn Valley Railway line, which isn't so much a road as a collection of ruts and ridges. They'd call it traffic calming anywhere else. In Jackfield it's a reminder that you can't excavate ad infinitum. In fact, reminders are everywhere if you know where to look. The original High Street for instance – originally a long, straight road used for running races before the war – comes to a premature end after 150 yards.

A couple of metal bars, themselves bent and twisted, mark the point where the asphalt plunges into what has become a woodland footpath. The terraced houses, along with the road, have vanished.

All that remains, a few hundred yards beyond the undergrowth, is the pub. Wouldn't you just know it! While everything around it slid relentlessly into the river, the Half Moon Inn still stands as firmly as it did more than a hundred years ago. The reason is that, unlike the houses that pressed against it, the hostelry was

Jackfield had more houses of ill-repute than the red light district of Amsterdam. The Severn Trow, now a bed and breakfast, is proud of its days as a brothel.

built on solid rock. Across the river stands another lone edifice, half-concealed by trees. This is the old Lloyds School, the last remnant of an adjoining hamlet called Lloyds, which also fell into the water.

What soon becomes obvious as you walk around this ghost town of a thousand cracks, where splintered roofs come into focus through the foliage, is that nature's reclamation has turned a beast into a beauty. Of all things, Jackfield has become a desirable place to live. If you want a holiday cottage here, you'll have to join the queue.

Pauline has even restored Jackfield's only surviving brothel 'cubicle', equipping it with a spanking new door and turning it into a small lavatory and washroom.

One of the 30 brothels is now a delightful B & B called The Severn Trow, run by Pauline Hannigan, for whom the extraordinary history of Jackfield has become a consuming hobby. I'm not surprised. For the first few years she and her late husband were reticent about the sordid history of their bankside home and workplace, before deciding to make a virtue of it – if you'll forgive the expression.

Pauline has even restored Jackfield's only surviving brothel 'cubicle', equipping it with a spanking new door and turning it into a small lavatory and washroom. Small is the operative word, by the way. Paying customers couldn't have got up to anything particularly gymnastic in what was little more than a broom cupboard, and they were watched by the brothel's Madam through a spy hole in the door. It's still there.

The Severn Trow, which bears a legend over the porch: 'Never mind the dog, beware of the owner', was as dilapidated as its morals when the Hannigans took over. The roof had caved in 25 years earlier, concealing a real treasure, even by Jackfield's standards. When they cleared away the debris, they found a stunning mosaic floor made of traditional one-inch square tiles in blue, red, black and white. Pauline explained that they must have been smuggled out of the factory piece-by-piece and assembled illegally, because there was no way the original owner could have afforded such a work of art. That's Jackfield for you. Thomas Telford's famous iron bridge at one end, an unsightly power station at the other, and lost in the middle, the village the cartographers forgot.

Broken castles, black and white houses, gurgling rivers and handsome hills
– no wonder Herefordshire's charm never wanes.

Off To Join The Circus

This is a love story. Several love stories, really. Toti for Nell, Carmen for Gerald and Nell for the circus. It was the circus which brought them all together and sustained their spirits on soaking wet days when the caravans were clogged with mud. Summers like 2000 would stretch anyone's patience. Heavy rain through July, August and September turned the travelling show business into a lottery. How would you like to move house, move animals and move two tons of big top every few days in conditions like that?

Don't answer. But the good days made up for it and there were plenty of those. Gifford's Circus played to full houses wherever it travelled across Oxfordshire, Gloucestershire and Wiltshire.

Long may it continue because not only is it extremely professional, it also symbolises everything that is good about imaginative private enterprise, as well as holding out hope for every romantic determined to pursue a dream.

It all began for Nell Stroud when her mother suffered a violent fall from horseback when Nell was 18. The fall wrecked her mother's life. It also changed Nell's for good. After a long period of caring for her immobilised parent, she ran away to join the circus – literally. Distant cousins in the USA ran a travelling show and Nell was quick to seize the opportunity. Things would never be quite the same again. Constantly moving from town to town, surrounded by trapeze artists and clowns, grooms and third generation show people, she immersed herself in their hard, marginalized and magical lives. Gradually that world became more real to her than the one she'd left behind.

"I was only there for a month and had to do all the menial jobs including mucking out the elephants," says Nell, "It was a fantastic feeling. I just fell in love with the circus life."

You could be forgiven for thinking this was an impressionable young fugitive talking, but you'd be wrong. Nell is a married woman in her thirties with an English degree from Oxford behind her and bills to pay like the rest of us. As we sat on the steps on her lovely old maroon and cream coloured caravan home I wondered if the circus venture might be a bit of a midlife crisis. "I sincerely hope not," she responded, "for one thing I'm not quite old enough and for another, the passion runs deeper than that."

The sky's the limit. Giffords have invested heavily in their dream to bring live entertainment to the village green. All the artistes are top class professionals.

Billy Smart's and Chipperfield's it ain't, but that's the joy of a small, intimate circus like Giffords, where love can strike at a moment's notice.

Nell married Toti Gifford, a wealthy landscape designer who sank all his money into the venture with barely a second thought. He wasn't eager to be interviewed but eventually relented. Why did *he* 'run' off to join the circus? " Because of my love for Nell. It also seemed a worthwhile thing to put back into country life something which has been lost."

Nell chips in with obvious pride: "It's not a penny of my money, neither is it inherited money. It's my husband's hard graft that has enabled it to happen. Sure, it could have put a big strain on the marriage but it's had exactly the opposite effect. We have so much fun you wouldn't believe it."

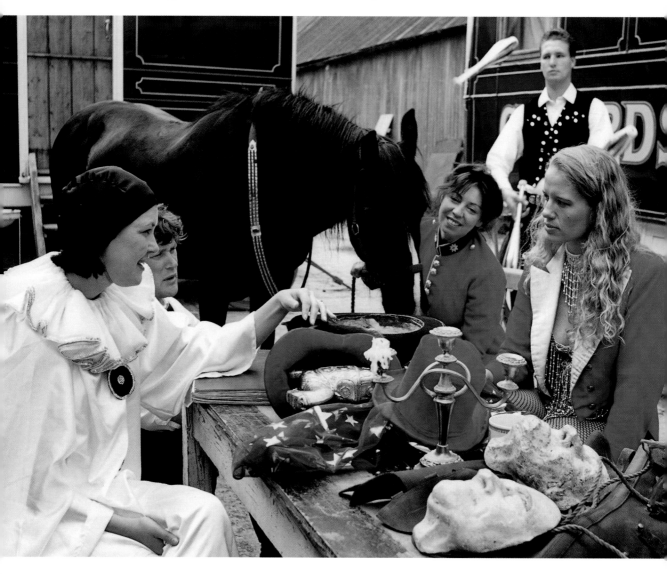

We were in Minchinhampton. It was early September. The back end of the summer circus calendar with only one more outing in Cheltenham before the show retired to its caravan-bound winter quarters until the following May. Minchinhampton's famous common looked great in the sun. The big tent in the middle could have appeared completely incongruous. Instead, nothing could have been more natural. Watching it take shape before opening night brought back vivid memories for me of visits to the circus with my parents and younger brother, when it transformed a scruffy piece of wasteground on the outskirts of Leicester into a noisy, flashing, pulsating wonderland.

In those days there were brown bears waving their huge paws at the trainer, elephants dancing to music, sea lions playing with beach balls, and, most impressive of all, lions growling on barstools as the tamer held them at bay with an upturned chair and a whip. None of it would be permitted today and I guess rightly so. Nevertheless, to kids who didn't give a thought to cruelty, it was miraculous. Mum and Dad drew the line at the man being shot out of a cannon, which was usually the finale. We had to leave before then, though there was never a convincing explanation. I told my brother it was because Mum couldn't stand the noise, which was probably right.

> *"Sure it could have put a big strain on the marriage but it's had exactly the opposite effect. We have so much fun you wouldn't believe it."*

I strolled into Minchinhampton to find out what the locals thought about the circus coming to town. A group of teenage girls sat in the butter market smoking cigarettes. One of them, who admitted to being 15, had a baby on her arm that could well have been hers. Were they going to the circus tonight? Blank faces. They didn't even know it was on. Nearby the organisers of the recent village flower show were up ladders removing their banner from the square. They, too, were negative. Miserable lot. Live entertainment on their own common and they couldn't be bothered. How village life has changed.

I'm happy to report that this inertia had no serious affect on the turnstiles. The circus was a sell-out before mid-afternoon. One hundred and seventy six seats gone. They were actually selling tickets to latecomers to stand outside the big top and peep through the gaps in the canvas. Backstage the dancers, gymnasts, trapeze artists and one taciturn but very good juggler were going through their paces in a relatively small space. A kaleidoscope of twisting bodies, flying clubs, dazzling costumes and pretty girls applying rouge to their already glowing cheeks.

Toti (don't know where he got the name) Gifford was Mr Cool. He bore a striking resemblance to Glenn Hoddle and was equally difficult to talk to. Every sentence had to be prised out of him because I suspect he didn't want to come across as the glory-seeking entrepreneur. He would rather Nell got all the attention. Nevertheless, he did grant me these few gems: "People say we were very brave to take this on, that it could have gone either way and we might have lost everything, but I'm a great believer in people's effort. With the amount of energy and enthusiasm that's been injected into the circus, it had to work. I knew it."

Even as he spoke the early crowds were arriving. Families, not just from Minchinhampton, but from several of the surrounding villages. Hardly surprising. It was the biggest thing to hit the area since the annual flower show and I know which of the two would be more likely to entice me. While they waited for the evening's performance, children were entertained on the only hand-driven merry-go-round I'd ever seen. Simple idea. The owner walked inside the rides with a piece of rope attached to the frame and Bob was your uncle.

Minchinhampton Common assumed a surreal air as the tent twinkled in the twilight. Over by the caravan, Nell and Toti were locked in an embrace any passer-by could have seen. They were obviously in love with each other and their 'baby'. That was why Gifford's

Circus was so successful. Love was the driving force. It shone through everything they did. What's more, it was highly contagious. Carmen Smith, who had been running the ticket office during the day, now adopted her other persona. This 25-year-old beauty with cropped hair and an iridescent smile had been a barmaid in London, earning extra pocket money as an occasional pub singer. She came across the circus by accident and thought 'why not?' Just like Nell, the magic entered her veins. And just like Nell, love blossomed on two fronts. She fell for the stage manager, Gerald Balding, who reciprocated.

Said Carmen: "I can't believe my luck. All these years I've wondered what to do with my life and now it's clear. I must have been destined to do this because it fulfils me in every way. Gifford's Circus is unique. Small, but all the better for it. We're a family. Everyone looks after everyone else. It's just wonderful." And the unmistakable glint in her eyes? "Yes, Gerald and I are in love. I have to pinch myself that all of this has really happened. How many people run away to join the circus and fall in love? It's what dreams are made of." You could say that again. Even the bearded, tousle-haired Gerald, a veteran of Nell's formative days on the American circuit, was rendered almost childlike by the euphoria of newly-found romance. "Love has struck and it's overpowering. Completely by chance, but the chemistry is right. These sorts of things happen in showbiz all the time, especially when a small group of people works closely together. Even so, it takes you by surprise when it happens to *you*."

By now one hundred and seventy six people were on the edge of their seats as the star of the show made her grand entrance. Nell, out of her denim skirt and into a dashing black number, blonde hair cascading down her back as the spotlight followed her sophisticated dressage routing on a chestnut mare. It was the only animal in the show. How big the ring became when the coloured lights played across it and the action began! I focussed in on Nell's face. She hadn't struck me as a showgirl at all. Quieter, more reserved in civilian life, but transformed now.

"People love the circus. They come back again and again. We have full-on groupies, like season-ticket holders, who have to see every performance. I feel very honoured because we go out of our way to give them something special. It's not a case of 'oh, here's Buster the Clown' and 'next, the high wire act.' We've spent six months designing the show. It's very carefully choreographed. The artists are all ultra-professional; the dancers are West End standard. If I say so myself, it's a really good circus."

Nell Gifford's life changed forever when her mother was paralysed after falling from a horse. Curiously it's on horseback she feels happiest.

The Bowthorpe Oak

We all know that from tiny acorns big oak trees grow, but that's a difficult concept to grasp as you stand dwarfed by the famous Bowthorpe Oak in Lincolnshire. It has the largest girth of any living oak in Britain – 39 feet, 1 inch.

How long did it take to grow to that size, I can hear you asking? The answer is just over one thousand years. A millennium.

Firm the roots into a small hole, add a handful of bonemeal, water well and wait for about a thousand years

For some reason it was hollowed out in the seventeenth century. But it's still in remarkably good shape – and still growing. According to legend, the Squire of Bowthorpe had a dinner party for 20 inside the tree. That's not hard to credit when you take tea and cakes with Ann Blanchard, whose family has owned the tree for three generations. There was plenty of room for a couple more tables, and just to prove the point we managed to squeeze an entire rugby team inside.

The Blanchard children converted it into a treehouse; lambs have sheltered there in snowy weather and a horse once had to be lifted out backwards when it got hopelessly stuck, having entered the 'front door' and attempted to exit by one of the portholes. Who knows how many foxes, rabbits, woodpeckers and squirrels have used it as a base over the centuries? If only trees could talk.

How Did It Get That Name? WIGWIG

I had to do a double-take, which is a trifle hazardous in a car. No, I hadn't imagined it, there really was a fingerpost pointing to Wigwig. This is getting silly, I thought. What earthly explanation could there be for that? Don't tell me this is the birthplace of the toupe or the Irish, as they say in cockney rhyming slang. Could it be that the whole village was bald?

I sent my fearless investigative reporter, Wendy Nelson, to get to the bottom of it – or top of it if you prefer. As is often the case, the truth was elusive. People who lived in the village (all 12 of them) hadn't given it a thought. (Incidentally, most of them had a good head of hair – I think!)

One guy remembered being teased at school; another was actually nicknamed 'Wigwig' by his classmates. The local farmer had a devil of a job convincing delivery people that he wasn't fooling. Apart from that, life in this fairly ordinary hamlet seemed unaffected by its fanciful and as yet unexplained moniker.

The closest we came was isolating its name in the Domesday Book of 1086 – Wigerwick – which didn't help us much. 'Wig' either referred to 'quaking ground' or was connected with insects (i.e. earwig) As far as we could tell there was no record of earth tremors and Wigwig didn't seem the most obvious place for an entomologists convention. There were no more wood lice, ladybirds or centipedes here than the next village (which incidentally went by the name of the Greek poet, Homer).

Perhaps a more logical explanation can be found in the Oxford Dictionary of Place Names. It suggests that a Saxon man called 'Wicga' farmed a 'wick' in this corner of Shropshire. How boring. Let's liven it up by suggesting that the farmer earned his name because he was the inventor of the first ginger 'syrup', the records of which have been lost in the mists of time.

The Wendover Recluse

Wendover is a colourful market town high in the Chiltern beech-woods of Buckinghamshire. A row of white, thatched 'Ann Boleyn' cottages first catches the eye as you approach the crossroads and clock tower at the bottom of the High Street. Brook House, on the other hand, makes you want to look away. What is arguably the best house in town, a Grade II listed, seven-bedroom farmhouse built on the Icknield Way in 1616 would probably be worth £1.5m in good condition. As it stands, Brook House is a local eyesore worth pulling down: boarded-up windows, crumbling masonry, pile upon pile of assorted debris on all sides and a shard of encrusted metal at the end of a wire where the doorbell used to be. Bijou residence it is not.

I'd driven past the place dozens of times and wondered what dark secrets lay behind its blackened windows. Why hadn't a developer bought it and restored it? Imagine my astonishment when I discovered that someone actually LIVED there! Was this a joke? How come there were never any milk bottles on the doorstep or lights at night? What do you mean, somebody *lives* there?

The shadow of a mouse running past the charred leg of a grand piano temporarily distracted me.

They told me about a reclusive old man who would call in at the pub up the road for warmth and a glass of whisky. They told me about the fire, which nearly killed him. Apparently he'd torn some wood panelling from the sitting room and lit a fire in the middle of the floor one sub-zero night. Firemen had saved his life.

I couldn't wait to meet him and eventually did. A smartly-dressed chap sporting a cravat and carrying a walking stick marched briskly past the clock tower towards the front gate of Brook House. Parking on a double-yellow line I leaped out of the car to greet him.

"Excuse me, Sir. Is this your house?"

He could have been rude but he wasn't.

"Of course it is. Why do you ask?"

"Because it's boarded up and I assumed it was empty."

"Vandals," he replied. Always trying to break in. That's why I board it up."

To my amazement, Ian Kirk, an 85-year-old former bomber pilot, prisoner of war and architect, agreed to let me see inside. It was an unforgettable experience. The hall was a burnt-out shell and smelled of smoke four years after the accident. The shadow of a mouse running past the charred leg of a grand piano temporarily distracted me.

"I've got a lot of those," said Mr Kirk. "and rats, especially in the kitchen."

The adjoining rooms, as far as I could make out in the gloom, were devoid of anything except one exhausted armchair and heaps of debris. The ceilings were hanging like Shredded Wheat.

My host lit a candle and announced defiantly that he had no heat, light and hardly any water. He drifted between the only two habitable (by his standards) rooms in this decaying mansion – a rubbish tip of a kitchen with no cooking facilities but a cold tap that dripped rather than ran – and a room at the top of the smoke-blackened stairs, where he spent most of his life huddled in a sleeping bag. His only luxury is a transistor radio picked out of a dustbin and permanently tuned to classical music. He wouldn't allow me to see upstairs. He said it was a mess!

I'd driven past Brook House scores of times and never seen a sign of life. Imagine my amazement when I discovered that someone lived behind those boarded-up windows.

Despite this appalling catalogue there has been some interest from potential buyers, with planning consent on the garden being a big attraction. An American visitor knocked on the door of Brook House recently and offered to move it brick by brick to an alternative site and erect half a dozen townhouses in its place. Mr Kirk's reaction?

"I told him the price was £5 million. That soon got rid of him." For the record, Mr Kirk bought the house for £9,500 from the lord of the manor in 1953.

Mr Kirk also claimed that the next-door neighbour – Tony Mogford, a farmer and justice of the peace – had tried to acquire the property. But Mr Mogford denies this. "When it was part of the Wendover Estate, my father-in-law rented it for a while," he says. "My wife has fond memories of being there when it was a really nice house. I wouldn't want the bother of it now, but when I suggested to Mr Kirk that he might be better off in a centrally heated bungalow, he thought I was trying to kick him out to develop the site."

I took Mr Kirk to the Red Lion, bought him a full English breakfast and asked him why he chose to live like this when he didn't have to. During the course of the conversation I began to understand how a well-educated, intelligent man could become so attached to such an apparently miserable existence – how independence could become more precious than comfort.

"Yes, it has been minus 10 degrees in the bedroom and I've gone to sleep wondering if I'd ever wake up. I always have, though. I put two corks under my pillow every night. They stop me getting cramp. It can get lonely but I've got my radio and I can always walk to the library."

The Wendover recluse opens up. Ian Kirk, an 85-year-old former bomber pilot with a twinkle in his eye, allows television cameras into his burned out wreck of a home for the first time.

Did he have a bathroom? He fudged that one. What about family? Only a distant relative in Australia, who never forgets his birthday on November 16th. His post is delivered to the flower shop. There was a long pause, during which I noticed that his cravat was coming undone, revealing small gashes where he had cut himself shaving in the dark.

Mr Kirk's only visitor over the past year or so has been Claire Pudney from the council's planning department. She told me that Aylesbury Vale could, in theory, buy Brook House, but the approach would have to come from Mr Kirk. "We can't be seen to interfere," she says. "People have the right to live the way they want. Nevertheless, I'd dearly love to work on a better solution. Mr Kirk may be eligible for a housing restoration grant but he'd have to be means-tested."

Meanwhile, the cost of restoring the house increases as each year goes by. It is already estimated at £250,000, but Mr Kirk's determination to stay rises with it. The mere suggestion of a residential home makes him see red.

"Don't talk about it. I had a friend who lived in a residential home. Very warm and comfortable with good food, but that's not living. Might as well be in prison. Do you know what I'd choose if I was granted a wish? A Blüthner grand piano."

"Ahead of electricity?"

"Any day of the week. Music can give you heat and light and a whole lot more."

He thanked me for breakfast and headed back home, stubborn to the end but seeking neither pity nor charity.

The Ghosts Of Minster Lovell

There are ghost stories... and there are ghost stories. Every house that predates Barratts seems to have one. In fact, visit a period house or stately home which *isn't* haunted and you feel cheated. Most of the stories wash over me because I've heard so many. But some demand closer scrutiny. Minster Lovell is one of them.

For a start the location is very atmospheric. A ruined abbey, so close to the meandering River Windrush in Oxfordshire as to be almost in it. Catch it in the oblique sunlight of an October afternoon when there isn't a soul around and you're in the mood to believe anything. I was first introduced to the place by the late Molly Harris, a Cotswold storyteller who loved the Windrush valley. She'd lived there all her life, probed its most intimate secrets and written books about its sparkling waters.

There's an uncanny similarity between the two famous ghost stories from Minster Lovell Hall, and yet the incidents are 300 years apart.

The story she retold while we strolled beneath the arches and around the ancient footings carried such passion that I couldn't help but lend an ear.

There are still people in the village who hear plaintive sobbing coming from the direction of Minster Lovell Hall at night. The identity of the tormented soul responsible is hard to pinpoint because there are two ghost stories attached to the Hall – uncannily similar in some respects yet unconnected and separated by three centuries. They involved innocent victims imprisoned in their own home.

Story one takes us back to the 1400's when the Lovells were one of the richest and most powerful families in Britain. To their consternation, the dashing young Francis Lovell, son and heir to the estate, betrayed the family tradition by siding with Richard III and fighting with the Yorkists at the Battle of Bosworth. Trouble began for Francis when the Lancastrians won. Suddenly he was a fugitive, fleeing from Leicestershire in an attempt to get back home – a cross-country ride fraught with peril.

They called off the search hoping that Genevieve would reveal herself before sundown and the newly-weds could enjoy their first night together. It didn't happen.

The game was almost up as he approached the River Trent, hotly pursued by the enemy cavalry. You know that old saying: "with one bound he was free"? Well, trapped between a rock and a hard place, Francis dug his spurs into the horse's flank and plunged into the river. The horse swam to the far bank and young Lovell completed the remainder of the journey to Oxfordshire without hindrance. Shades of Butch Cassidy and Sundance.

There was a room at the top of Minster Lovell Hall only Francis Lovell knew about. He resolved to spend as many days as it took concealed in the garret to throw the bloodthirsty Lancastrians off the scent. Little could he have known that he would never see daylight again.

Installing himself in the room with only his dog and a few possessions for company, Francis issued strict instructions to his manservant to bring food once a day and reveal nothing to anyone about his place of hiding.

The plan seemed simple and effective enough. For several weeks it worked well. Then the servant vanished. Maybe there was a quarrel over something. Maybe he was killed by the Lancastrians for not disclosing information about the upper class fugitive. The story goes cold for 250 years by which time most people have forgotten all about it. The assumption was that Francis must have been put to the sword after the Battle of Bosworth and never made it back to Minster Lovell at all.

It's the second half of the 1600's before the truth is uncovered by accident. The hall is scheduled for renovation and the builders move in. Everything goes to plan until they come to remove the old fireplace upstairs. Imagine their horror and dismay when they find the skeletal remains of a young soldier with his dog at his feet...

About 50 years later came a second, even more tragic discovery. The next ghost story concerns another Lovell son and heir, William, who married a pretty and spirited young woman called Genevieve. As you'd expect, the wedding was followed by a sumptuous reception at Minster Lovell Hall to the accompaniment of music and dance. As was their wont, the gathering ate and drank themselves almost stationary and were no doubt preparing themselves for another session when the feisty Genevieve decided to spice up the evening. This is where the love story begins to fall apart, although none of the guests, sober or legless, could have anticipated the sequel.

Genevieve coaxed her new husband away from the bacchanalia, insisting the couple play hide and seek in the grounds. William began to count as his loved one darted through the house and grounds looking for the perfect hiding place. With several hundred acres of parkland, lakes and forests, the possibilities were endless. Finally, Genevieve decided to explore the hidden corners of the vast building.

As he embarked on the search William was in good spirits. He sensed victory around every bend in the river, every corner of estate. After an hour of fruitless searching he became at first irritated, then alarmed. He called out to her that the game was over and to come out immediately, her parents were gertting upset. Silence.

Summoning friends and family together, he formed groups and began to systematically search the grounds and ransack the house. Half demented with worry, William charged around the gardens, calling her name at the top of his voice. No response. They searched until it was too dark to see.

By daybreak the groups had reformed. By this time they realised that something was very wrong. Had she slipped and fallen into the River Windrush? Perhaps she had been kidnapped?

Those who knew Genevieve well suggested a less ingenuous theory. Just hours after taking her vows she had been seen flirting outrageously with an unknown male guest. She was a beautiful but wilful young woman. Her parents had put pressure on her to marry advantageously. Had the game of Hide and Seek been carefully arranged to allow her to elope with a lover after fulfilling her parents demand?

It was this thought that haunted William. According to Molly Harris's version of the legend, he was inconsolable and died shortly afterwards of a broken heart. But how many coroners have ever come up with that as an acceptable conclusion? None to my knowledge. More likely that William took his own life. History denies us the pathologist's report so we'll move on to the dénouement.

Ten or so years later, Minter Lovell Hall was due some more renovation work and the mystery was solved. Sounds familiar, doesn't it? Just as the stonemasons had found Francis Lovell's remains earlier that century, so the new builders were in for an awful shock. There, in one of the turrets close to Francis' old hiding place, was an oak chest. No-one could remember having seen it before. The builders forced it open at the family's request. Staring up at them was the haunted face of Genevieve, now just a collection of bones shrouded in her wedding costume. The poor girl had climbed into a self-locking chest and cried in vain for someone to release her. At least she won the game!

So whose is the plaintive sobbing which still echoes around the village? It could belong to Francis, to Genevieve or to William – or to members of the Lovell family. If you're ever down Minster Lovell way, call in... and listen.

I must confess I didn't hear anything unusual, although there are still people in the nearby village who hear plaintive sobbing at night.

The Rutland Panther

If there's anything better than a good ghost story, or rumours of a Martian landing, it's a dangerous wild animal on the loose. And if the creature's range is restricted to the rolling prairies of England's smallest county, the plot thickens, the excitement reaches fever pitch. Nobody likes to be a party pooper at times like this. Heaven knows, life can be humdrum enough. So when a couple of dozen people claim to have seen a foreign beast prowling around the farmland, for goodness sake believe them. I did. The Rutland Panther is out there.

So it is with the Rutland Panther. David Spencer should know. He was considered perfectly normal until one dark January morning in the early 90's when he was about to open his garden gate to take the dog for a walk. Neither his life nor that of his long-suffering family, have been the same since. This is his chilling story.

"I heard a pounding noise coming from the field opposite. It sounded like a horse, but the animal I could make out in the dim light wasn't big enough to be a horse. The creature came closer and closer. I ruled out dog, fox and badger while realising that it was on a collision course with me. If it didn't attack me, it would have to jump over me!"

David shouted at the mystery animal, upon which it swerved across the road, too close

"I was shaking with fear. Lots of people don't believe me but I've seen it, they haven't."

for comfort. He continued: "That's when I saw its long tail as it bounded along almost in slow motion. There was a strong smell of ammonia at the same time. The animal disappeared into the distance, plain as the nose on your face. I have no proof that it ever existed but I'd heard it, seen it and smelt it."

Unless, of course, ammonia was the smell of fear in his own subconscious. Whether or no, his close encounter that winter morning adjusted David's focus. He began Operation Black Panther, which shows no sign of running out of steam. The Control Centre is the family home in Knossington. His office looks like Field Marshall Montgomery's during El Alemain: Maps, charts, cuttings, magnifying glasses and publications from around the world. Rutland had become his Serengeti. David Attenborough would have been mightily impressed.

Once the ball was rolling, the momentum swiftly gathered. Others reported sightings practically every passing week. His table-mounted Ordnance Survey map of the area sparkled with panther sightings all recorded since his garden-gate confrontation. In all there were 40; some reported to the police, all co-ordinated by David.

There were two major concentrations. One stretched from Oakham to Leicester, to the west of Rutland Water; the other was in the Ketton/Edith Weston region to the east of the county, with virtually no sightings in between. David therefore concluded that we were faced with not one black panther, but TWO. With that realisation came the distinct possibility that the Beast of Rutland was multiplying.

Now, the story goes that the creatures must have been set free after the Wild Animals Act was introduced in 1976. It tightened up on the proliferation of exotic pets in so-called menageries that had been springing up around the UK. Until '76, any Tom, Dick or Harry could jump on the safari bandwagon. I remember reporting on an eccentric Black Country builder who kept a fully grown male lion in his garden. How daft can you get?

As soon as the practice was outlawed, the English countryside resembled a scene from Jungle Book, as tigers, bears, wallabies and chimpanzees were released surreptitiously into the wild. Along with the odd escapee from zoos and private collections, they went on to create a new branch of British wildlife.

Visible proof – or is it? The Rutland Panther caught on camera by an amateur sleuth. Surely there can't be any doubt?

Back at Control HQ, David was studying his grid references before setting off with his son, Nigel, on another expedition across the Rutland/Leicestershire border. They'd drawn a blank since David and his dog shared that 'ammonia moment' nearly ten years earlier. In the same way that you can't persuade a gold prospector to give up once he's got the scent in his nostrils, there was no reining back the Spencers. Father and son spend hours searching the hedgerows for clues and mum doesn't seem to mind. Says Shirley: "It's become a mission in their lives, but at least it gives them a shared interest." She is, in effect, a panther widow.

There have been sightings as far away as Kettering and beside a dual carriageway in Leicester. The most vivid piece of evidence, however, was supplied by a Rutland nurse, Samantha Dodd, who was returning home to Normanton from the night shift at about 8 o'clock one morning, when she had the fright of her life. Let her tell her story.

"I heard this rustle in the bushes and all of a sudden a cat came out. It was big. Very big. I was gobsmacked."

Samantha had stopped the car not far from the half-submerged Normanton church, a local landmark. Feeling unable to drive on, she locked the doors from the inside.

"It walked around my car but it didn't take much notice of me. There was no question of it being frightened. It sniffed the bonnet then walked off up the road. I followed it for a while then it disappeared through the hedge. I was shaking with fear. I couldn't believe it. Lots of people don't believe me but I've seen it, they haven't."

How can you doubt her sincerity? In any case, I've seen the video evidence. It was gathered by an amateur sleuth not far from the fields around Knossington and it shows quite clearly a black panther on the prowl. The parting shot, as the animal lopes off stage left, leaves you in no doubt that this is the genuine article. Big, long-striding with that unmistakeable tail.

Our mini-expedition led us eventually to the quarry at Ketton Cement Works. Evidence of dinosaurs, mammoths and sabre-tooth tigers you'd expect, but panthers? Not usually. Patricia Stewart-Mogg, a receptionist at the works, was in no doubt.

Tangible proof – or is it? David Spencer examines the plaster cast of what he believes is a panther's footprint at Ketton Cement Works.

"I saw the cat walk from behind the canteen towards the gate and the allotments beyond. It was as casual as you like, taking no notice of cars coming and going in the car park, or the noise from the canteen. It was black with a long tail and definitely feline. I rushed out to have a look but it had gone."

David Spencer's resolve hasn't wavered. He thinks it's important to try to build up a picture of the panther's movements and eating habits. What is it killing for food? Sheep? There have been no complaints from farmers. At the cement works David showed us his 'piece de resistance'. It consisted of two plastic casts of panther paw prints from the quarry. There are no claw marks which, in David's submission, rules out the possibility of a dog. A cat's claws are protected as it walks, so there's little chance of their being exposed in a print. Exciting stuff, though our missionary is philosophical:

"This is about as close as I'll ever get to the Rutland Panther. I hope so, anyway!"

How Did It Get That Name?   WYRE PIDDLE

There it sits, minding its own business, on the banks of the River Avon near Evesham. A stone bridge, a pub called the Angler and one or two half-timbered houses. Nothing showy. And yet Wyre Piddle is the subject of scorn and derision across the land. After all these years it still raises a titter in polite circles.

At the turn of the century two spinsters, who ran the village in the absence of a lord of the manor, did their damndest to shorten the name to 'Wyre'. They deemed it infra-dignitatum, not to say downright rude. Gathering around them an army of disgruntled Victorian ladies, the sisters marched on County Hall to make their objections known. The then chairman chastised them for being so precious, told them he wouldn't change the name even if they bribed him and bid the biddies good day.

He was later heard to say that if anything, they should drop the prefix and keep the 'Piddle' because it was more ancient in origin. In fact it derives from the Dutch word 'piddel' meaning marshy ground. Sorry to disappoint you, but there's nothing naughty about Wyre Piddle, even though it was once the home of a nappy factory (perfectly true).

For the record, Piddle is the name given to a stream which feeds into the Avon a couple of miles away at Pershore. Wyre is broad Worcestershire for 'weir'. So there you have it.

The Antiques Rogue Show

Forget Broadway, push Burford to the back of your mind, don't even think about Stow on the Wold. The antiques capital of England is an unglamorous, working class town in north Staffordshire where men still queue for a haircut on Saturday mornings.

Leek has seen better days. Prosperous days for the silk mill owners. Fulfilling days for the workforce who hardly knew the meaning of unemployment. When the mills, the mines and the potteries closed, Leek discovered the spirit-sapping nature of that awful word. To be out of work destroyed your self-esteem. You either festered in self-pity or you re-invented yourself. Leek chose the latter.

Thousands of square feet of derelict mills have been transformed into warehouses. First one antique dealer sprang up, then another, and another. Like Hay on Wye with its bookshops, Leek realised that to make the town worth visiting it had to have several dealers specialising in different aspects of the trade. Now there are 75 of them, along with sundry polishers, restorers and pine strippers.

People from the highly-polished galleries of the Cotswolds, where Des O'Connor was once turned away for wearing jeans, would shudder, because Leek is rough and ready. But the turnover is immense. Where it might take Peter Kiel in Broadway months to sell an expensive item which occupies lots of floor space, Stephen Hibberts will get rid of a vanload of material in four days at the outside. That's

Once a famous mill town on the edge of the Staffordshire Moorlands, Leek went through several traumas before reinventing itself.

Limelight

Heart of the Country made history in 1997 when we reactivated a lime kiln for the first time in 75 years. Quite spectacular it was too. I hadn't realised what a remarkable substance limestone is, nor how the expression 'in the limelight' came about. Laura and I were soon to find out.

Opening up an old lime kiln on a hillside near Buxton was largely thanks to a local historian and quarryman called Claude Fearns, who said it was the fulfilment of his lifetime's ambition. He'd only lived in the area for 69 years so why his history society couldn't have got around to it before we suggested the idea, I'll never know. Once we provided the impetus, Claude and his colleagues located a suitable disused kiln and spent most of the night preparing it for our experiment.

William Pickford knocked down half a mile of dry stone walls on his estate so that he could build a mammoth lime kiln. It was the start of his removals business.

Let me explain our purpose. I'd read a lot about Peak District farmers burning limestone to produce a fertiliser, which turned their soil into gold dust, spurring on the brassicas to extraordinary sizes. Lime is still widely used today on farms. What I couldn't visualise was how they set fire to stone and why the resulting lime was so volatile as to be positively explosive.

Claude dispelled all my misgivings. His father had been nastily burned when a small amount of lime worked its way inside his shirt and reacted with sweat to scorch his chest. For that reason, Claude had been forbidden to go anywhere near a lime kiln. Until now.

While the logs crackled gleefully and the stones warmed up, we discovered that lime was also responsible for the birth of the furniture removal business, strange though it sounds. Pickfords, the biggest operators

"Don't go too near," Claude advised in a thick Derbyshire twang. "It's extremely dangerous. Put your hand in there and it'd soon be down to the bones."

in the UK, lived at King Sterndale Hall in north Derbyshire. They were a wealthy family who owned the nearby Groyt Quarry. The entrepreneurial William Pickford had covered, horse-drawn wagons, ferrying limestone to London to pave Regent Street and most of London's West End. The journey took days but William made sure the wagons were full of other materials on the way back. A national freight movement had begun.

Back in the High Peak, William was quick to realise the market potential of lime. He even knocked down half a mile of dry stone walling at King Sterndale Hall to build a mammoth lime kiln called 'a layered pudding'. The magical white dust was carried to farmers across the Peak by packhorse and that's how the removals business began.

The risk to the horses from such a venture was brought home to us when Claude filled an aluminium bowl with chunks of limestone allowed to go cold after being retrieved from the kiln, and poured a can of cold water over them. On the face of it, a harmless-enough activity. You should have seen what happened. Within 20 or 30 seconds the cold water was boiling as the lime started to dissolve. Within 2 minutes, the whole lot had turned into a frothing white syrup as the lime absorbed the water.

"Don't go too near," Claude advised in his thick Derbyshire twang, "It's extremely dangerous. Put your hand in there and it'd soon be down to the bones." I soon

The effect of pouring cold water on burned limestone was staggering. In seconds we had a boiling froth which could have been lethal.

Swanning Around On The Thames

I remember when cygnet was a once-a-year banquet at my old Cambridge College. It seems remarkable that swan was originally bred for the table.

You could call it an excuse for a day out on the river with a generous pub lunch and a few beers thrown in. The truth is, it takes much more than a day and behind the pageantry lies a serious purpose.

It's called Swan-Upping. Each July for well over 800 years a group of sailors are appointed to weigh, measure and record the new crop of cygnets on the Thames. They travel in traditional Thames skiffs marked 'Vinters' or 'Dyers' from Hampton Court to Windsor, to Henley, through Goring and Streatley, past Wallingford and onto Abingdon. Newcomers watch nonplussed by this most eccentric of English customs. Regulars line the banks and the bridges for a glimpse of the flotilla, which signals another landmark in the summer calendar, like Wimbledon or Royal Ascot.

The day I joined the Swan-Uppers was perfect. Hot sunshine illuminated this majestic waterway; brilliant blue damsel flies hovered as though recovering their bearings before darting off faster than the eye could follow them; the scent of limes and willows and flower displays on passing cruisers hung in the air. The normal sounds of the river were punctured by broad cockney accents as the Swan-Uppers tried to round up a group of swans only to lose them under the overhanging trees and the stately reeds. I caught the odd swear word, which surprised me because these chaps were working exclusively for Her Majesty the Queen. It surprised some of the onlookers too. They weren't supposed to be within earshot!

The annual cygnet count dates back to the 12th century, when swan was on the menu in royal circles and select households. Someone had to keep an eye on the chicks, which all belonged to the Crown and would be needed for the autumn banquets. I actually recall seeing Cygnet St John on the menu at my old college in Cambridge. Not for commoners like me, I hasten to add, but at some important gathering of university dignitaries, the precise details of which escape me.

Swan was bred for the table in medieval times because it was easy to keep and provided a good source of nutrition. As time went on, it was superseded by the ubiquitous turkey.

Back on the river David Barber, complete with his captain's hat and his scarlet jacket, was 'El Supremo'. His afternoon job was running a boat-building company on the Thames, but for now he was Chief Swan Marker, an honour he took very seriously, although he did raise a smile under cross examination.

He was responsible for all the swans in the UK where the Queen wanted to exercise the 'Royal Prerogative Rights of Ownership.' Furthermore, he was charged with delivering the results of their survey to Buckingham Palace by the end of the week.

The Queen doesn't like swans very much. At least not for breakfast. She had a flock removed from her lake because they got in the way of the royal flamingos.

"Do you think the Queen will ever read it?" I asked. David permitted himself a wry smile. "There's a possibility, but I couldn't guarantee it." My guess is that it would be well down her holiday reading list. The fact is that HRH doesn't actually like swans very much. At least not for breakfast. She had a flock of them removed from her lake at Buckingham Palace because they were getting in the way of the royal flamingos. A little-known nugget of trivia I collected from one of the Swan-Uppers who requested that his anonymity should be preserved because treason carried a stiff penalty.

The same fellow told me that Prince Andrew went Swan-Upping with them back in 1975. He allegedly preferred tea to beer but got stuck into the jellied eels for lunch. "Whenever we see him, he reminds us of it," said my informant, though I couldn't help wondering how often the two would cross paths.

Lunch had been a grand affair at the Ann Boleyn Hotel at Staines, built by Henry VIII to entertain the second of his eight wives on her excursions up and down the Thames. Then he chopped her head off. She'd probably been eating him out of swan. All I can say is that it's a good job the boatmen had broken the back of the exercise in the morning. The afternoon was destined to be somewhat sleepier. I put it to David, the CSM, that Swan-Upping might just, in some quarters, be perceived as an excuse to dress up and go on a pub crawl.

"No," he replied, masterfully. "We take this extremely seriously. Of course we look after the ceremonial side but that shouldn't obscure the conservation aspect. We're monitoring the swans hopefully to keep numbers up."

Rounding up trhe cygnets is no easy task – especially when you've been on the bottle.
Some of those captured before lunch would have had every chance of escaping *after* lunch.

A fair point. I had earlier called at Dot Beeson's nearby swan sanctuary, where the vet was removing a fisherman's hook from a bird's throat at the same time as a cygnet with severe mink damage was arriving at A & E. The cygnet was immediately put on a drip as Dot reminded me that in the late 1980's, the swan population of the Thames was nearly wiped out. Their natural enemies were anglers, mink and gangs of youths who appeared to take a delight in torturing them. She'd just had a mutilated cygnet die at the sanctuary and there was a break in her voice as she recounted the tale.

On the river, Professor Chris Perrins from Oxford University, was in charge of the weighing and measuring. The boatman had skilfully ambushed a large family of swans, manoeuvred them towards the bank before seizing them in swift but careful movements, which belied their lunchtime activities, and lifting them into the skiff. I was interested to pursue the theory that swans were the only birds that genuinely mated for life. Since this was July 15th, the day that Prince Charles and Lady Diana announced their divorce, the subject was apposite. How the Queen must have wished that one of her offspring, at least, could mimic the swan.

The new crop of cygnets are numbered and recorded on behalf of the Queen who expects the results delivered to her door by Christmas each year. I wonder if she ever reads them?

I was disabused of the fidelity notion at once. Said the professor: "It's a myth. You present me with any curious human relationship and I can match it with the social behaviour of the swan. They split up and run off with another bird. Mothers pair up with sons and fathers with daughters. It's so incestuous you wouldn't believe it." So much for that theory then. Royalty had probably been mimicking the swan for centuries and I hadn't even realised.

Dot Beeson's testimony was less damning: "In 15 or 16 years of dealing with swans I've only seen two cases of unfaithfulness. Both mothers had two nests on the go at the same time." Shock horror.

But had Dot, David or the professor ever tasted swan or come across anyone who still dined on the creature? Dot and the academic shook their heads furiously. David said he wouldn't eat swan on principle but didn't rule out the possibility that someone, somewhere might be less fussy.

That said, the Chief Swan Marker gathered his fleet in the lock, waited until the whisky had been ceremonially poured into glasses not much bigger than thimbles and raised a toast to the Queen. I made my excuses and left as the bottom lock opened, releasing Vintners and Dyers to continue their round-up in the direction of Henley. I had learned a lot about swans and a little about the Royal Family, not all of it fit for publication.

Partners In Rhyme

I was lucky enough to meet the author Laurie Lee in the summer of '95. He was frail and he stuttered and it was clear from his puffy features that drink had taken rather a heavy toll. He was however every inch the incurable romantic poet treating the English language as though it were porcelain whenever he spoke. Each sentence had a cadence; each adjective was carefully chosen from a rich thesaurus he'd developed over years of writing.

He allowed himself half a pint of beer as we sat outside his favourite watering hole in Stroud, enjoying the sunshine and watching the human traffic. The creator of 'As I walked out one Midsummer morning' was mine for the afternoon.

We'd met to talk about Sheepscombe. In fact, he'd agreed to accompany me to this idiosyncratic Gloucestershire village 750 feet up in the Cotswolds, where Laurie's fellow poet and drinking companion, the late Frank Mansell excelled in both disciplines. I'd read about him in 'Cider with Rosie':-

The craziest cricket field in England? Fielders on the boundary could only see the top of the batsman's head because of the dizzy contours at Sheepscombe. Laurie Lee said "Next to Slad it's the place for which I have the deepest affection."

"At first only the outfield was visible. Then you'd see the top of Frank's cap and his flushed face and great heaving shoulders until gradually, like a galleon, he'd come billowing into view and loose his fast, furious ball like a shot out of a cannon."

Cricket was the other passion shared by the two friends. Laurie had paid £600 for a slice of limestone hilltop that he gave to Sheepscombe so that on summer weekends the crack of leather on willow would forever echo through this part of the county.

You had to see Sheepscombe's cricket ground to believe it. Laurie called it 'playing sport on the back of a pony' – the pavilion situated between the animal's ears and the pitch briefly occupying a hanging plateau before plunging sharply into a wooded valley. A more improbable arena you could scarcely imagine. Its crazy contours meant that fielders on the bottom boundary could only see the batsman's cap. They had to rely on radar to stand any chance of anticipating the ball coming in their direction, by which time it was probably too late to stop it. What's more, a glider pilot experiencing some mechanical trouble over the village once crash-landed in the woods because it looked safer than the wicket!

Said Laurie: "It's theirs for as long as they want it. If they stop playing cricket I hope they'll turn it into a children's sports field in honour of my mother who was brought up in Sheepscombe. She worked with her grandfather in The Plough where she was the only one who could control the rough cider drinkers. My uncles also lived there. Next to Slad where I was brought up, it's the place for which I have the deepest affection."

Laurie took another sip of beer from his half pint jug, which reminded me of my old boss Roland Orton at Leicester News Service, the only other person I've known to order a half, let alone drink it from a glass with a handle. I wondered at Laurie's moderation.

He went on to tell me how Frank Mansell terrorised the Stroud league with his aggressive bowling. There was one occasion when Sheepscombe beat Birdlip after decades of trying. Frank did the trick, claiming eight victims for a mere eleven runs.

Sadly with us no more. Laurie Lee epitomised everything good about the countryside. His books and his poems are as Cotswoldian as a dry stone wall yet he handled the English language as though it were porcelain.

But Frank the demon paceman was a multi-coloured character for whom cricket was only one of life's joys. This is how Laurie remembered him best:-

"You never knew where you'd run into him. He could be up a telegraph pole or emerging from a hole in the road spouting poetry. He wrote verse about the area he loved, country poetry which was never precious. Poetry as rough as a dry stone wall covered with moss."

The two of them published Frank's first collection themselves. It was called "Cotswold Ballads." They had it printed in Stonehouse and delivered copies in cardboard boxes to the local pubs. They called back a week later to collect the money and discovered to their amazement that 2,000 copies had been snapped up. "That's a lot of poetry books. People wanted it and Frank obliged," said Laurie.

"Frank's unforgiving phantom, champion man that he was, is sitting on that seat watching every move they make."

A bit of detective work on my part turned up one poem which had been set to music. "When the rain falls" surprised me. A lovely folk tune sweetly sung by a young woman nobody in the village could identify. Pity. She had a fine voice. Also on vinyl, much the worse for wear, was another verse read by Frank himself. Although it was written in the 60's it has a resonance today as property-seekers from London and Birmingham snap up desirable homes in the Cotswolds for their weekend getaways:

"You say you'll pay ten thousand pounds
For this old house and bit of ground.
You like these hills and have it planned
To settle down on Cotswold land.
Well come you in and sit you down.
You would-be buyer from the town
And listen to me while I tell
The reasons why I will not sell."

Laurie Lee went on to become famous whereas Frank died in virtual anonymity, a humble lineman, cricketer and rural poet. From a sporting point of view there was no comparison between the two. "I would have loved to play the way he did," Laurie confessed. "I was good in the slips, though it didn't make me friends with anyone. I remember the Liberal candidate from Bristol coming to Sheepscombe to show-off. A flash young man who wanted to be the centre of attention. He couldn't handle Frank's bowling. I caught him in the slips – a spinning ball I was pleased to hold onto. The Liberal candidate exploded with rage, calling me a 'bloody peripatetic poet!' and complaining that he came here to bat, not to be caught by me. He marched to the pavilion in a fearful huff and smashed his bat on the steps."

The day we filmed for Heart of the Country I had the dubious pleasure of witnessing the first-ever televised hat-trick at Sheepscombe, unfortunately inflicted upon them by Frampton on Severn. No-one could believe, that on the one day in its hundred-odd year history, that television cameras were there, the home team crumbled as three wickets fell in three balls. It was some time afterwards that I noticed a black greyhound reclining behind the scoreboard, and remembered something Laurie had told me. Apparently Frank Mansell dreaded seeing a black

Laurie and Frank Mansell plan their next adventure. Between them they sold 2,000 copies of Frank's poetry in local pubs.

dog on the way to the cricket ground. As far as he was concerned it was curtains for the team. Time and again he was proved right.

Curious thing about Frank. One of his poems is called "In Sheepscombe let me lie." A bench at the boundary's edge bears the same inscription. And yet he isn't buried in the village. He doesn't lie there at all.

"Ah," said Laurie, "but his spirit does. That bench is haunted by him. He barracks the players when they're doing idiotic things. He never for a moment forgave bad play. Frank's unforgiving phantom, champion man that he was, is sitting on that seat watching every move they make."

Frank died in 1979 at the age of 60. Laurie Lee died in March 1997 at the age of 82. Sheepscombe misses them both.

Youlgreave Goes It Alone

In the Derbyshire Dales, where men eat oatcakes for breakfast and fight tug-of-war battles in the Sunday league, there's a village called Youlgreave. Proud, independent, stubborn. So stubborn that when Severn Trent offered to help it out of a little local difficulty with its water supply the villagers chorused in unison: "Naff off."

This healthy disregard for authority is something we've all wanted to display at one time or another. The difference is that Youlgreave could hold up its metaphorical two fingers from a position of strength. Since 1860 when Youlgreave Waterworks Ltd was formed, the village had been more or less self-sufficient when it came to H_2O. The kettles and bathtubs of this predominantly mining population were filled from local supplies. Until the 1990's Severn Trent's only responsibility was to pick up the shortfall.

"I can tell it from Severn Trent water blindfold," he boasted. "It's purer and sweeter. There's now't like it."

Then came a couple of bad droughts. The underground streams began to dry up and YWL was in trouble. Harry Holland, the company chairman, reflected: "It got so bad we had to *buy* water from Severn Trent. We nearly went bankrupt." Why, I wondered, didn't the official water authority simply take over?

"Oh, they would have done," Harry went on. "We had an Extraordinary General Meeting and the village decided unanimously that it wanted to keep its independence at all costs. We'd been enjoying our own water for 140 years and we weren't about to stop."

Youlgreave recovered from the glitch to consolidate its position as one of only three communities in England which provides all its own water. It comes from beneath the rocks and is processed at a small bunker in the corner of a field – the Youlgreave Water Treatment Plant. From the outside it says DIY but on the inside it's an impressive collection of wires, pumps and gauges which cost several thousand pounds to install. It's here that chlorine is added to the water, under the

It's what lies beneath the surface that *really* matters. Youlgreave's underground streams produce 40 million gallons a year.

watchful gaze of John Wardle, a local plumber, who claims that Youlgreave's water is supreme.

"I can tell it from Severn Trent Water blindfold," he claimed. "It's purer and sweeter. There's nowt like it." The Waterworks has an agreement with the Environment Department to extract more than 40 million gallons a year, easily enough to provide for its 1250 inhabitants and probably enough to supply surrounding villages, too.

What has made a difference is the reopening of Moorstone Mine, which has brought an extra 20 million gallons on stream. It's a sensitive area. A dozen young men from the village were killed in a pit disaster there in the 1930's. Youlgreave has always known about the additional supplies of water at the mine but didn't want to reopen old wounds. Almost 70 years on, the pain had faded enought.

E.L.S.255-3. The fountain, Youlgreave.

I visited the pithead, (now lost in the woods) where Harry unlocked the grill over the main shaft. It had been untouched for years. Waterworks engineers still use the original winch to lower themselves into the mine. Tapping into this abundant source has increased the rates from £95 to £100 a year to pay for the bank loan. Nobody seems to mind.

The stone fountain where women queued at 6am to fill their buckets and brought their knitting to while away the time.

In the village square, protected by iron railings, stands a circular stone fountain where women used to queue at six o'clock in the morning to fill their buckets. The fountain, dated 1829 and now out of use, was always padlocked overnight to make sure it was full next morning when the Waterkeeper arrived to open up. The tap was small so it was a time-consuming business filling up. Women would bring their knitting and the fountain became a focal point for gossip as well as a bring-and-buy stall for homemade produce. The original parish pump.

Before I left, I had to challenge John Wardle's idle boast. We dispensed with the blindfold but I presented him with two identical-looking glasses of water. He tasted the first and immediately announced that it was Youlgreave water, without even trying the second. What's more, he was right.

The Nervous Twitcher

Lee Evans sensed that he was in trouble the moment he turned away from the altar. His frenzied friends were trying to tell him something. Lip-reading being a particular forte, he deciphered the message in double-quick time and managed to conceal it from his new bride. The gist of it was that Isabelline had turned up. Today of all days. He could hardly believe it. Often in the past he'd sailed close to the wind. Now he was navigating, part-willingly, into the teeth of a cyclone.

There was no mistaking the name being mouthed as he walked back down the aisle: Isabelline. Two thousand five hundred miles from Lake Baikal just to be near him, and he'd gone and got married! How do you ignore an appointment with destiny? On the other hand, how do you explain your imminent departure to a wife of precisely 10 minutes? The signatures on the register were still moist.

Lee wrestled with his conscience for a good 30 seconds. Dreaming up an alibi was more difficult. But a delay might be fatal. That's when he shifted into overdrive. When there's no time for thought, allow the heart to rule the head and the con-

"Her indoors versus a tasty foreign bird? No contest."

sequences will take care of themselves. In the melee of guests, ushers and photographers that traditionally separates the ceremony from the reception, our nimble-footed groom slipped surreptitiously away.

Gunning his Cavalier towards the M4, he was seized by a frisson of regret – but was at once heartened by the certainty of a greater love. Her indoors versus a tasty foreign bird? No contest.

On the pretext of popping home to change into his lounge suit for the speeches and the telegrams, Lee back-tracked on the troth he'd just plighted and took the first steps towards divorce. It was 115 miles to Portland Bill and he would be gone for four hours. His rationale? "The Isabelline shrike is a very rare bird. You might see it once in a hundred years if you're incredibly lucky. For it to appear on a Dorset peninsula was a fluke. My wife would still be there in the morning. The shrike probably wouldn't." No contest.

The first Mrs Evans will take no consolation from the fact that Lee placed his marriage in immediate jeopardy for the sake of "a little brown job." That's all the shrike was, after all. I first met Lee on the Scillies last October. We were straining our eyes to see a northern parula nestling in a group of elms on the island of St Agnes. The little warbler had been diverted by fierce winds from its migratory route between the USA and Venezuela.

My cameraman and I agreed that a needle in a haystack would have been substantially easier to locate and 400 birders were growing rattier by the minute. All they could see were leaves. But although deprived of the use of one eye (the legacy of a motorway pile-up in heavy fog when he was in his late teens), Lee was quickly onto it.

Warm autumn sun glinting on the crucifix chained to his ear, binoculars strung superfluously over his chest, flecks of grey in his designer stubble. Beside him, his new girlfriend, Carmel. Slightly reluctantly, she'd become a convert, learning early on that the only way to keep the relationship alive was to play Lee's game.

"He won't marry me because his first wife gave him such a hard time. She thought she could change him. I don't even try. Lee's what he is. Take him or leave him. Even though there isn't really any place for me in his world and even though it drives me mad when the pager wakes us up every morning, I stay around. Don't really know why. I suppose I must love him."

"She's very understanding," said Lee, after a moment's deliberation. "She knows what I'm all about. I'm lucky." Had he gone soft or what? Before I had time to work that one out, he launched into a running commentary on the day's tick (birdwatcher-speak for the specimen recorded that day): "There he goes. Beautiful. Custard yellow with a chestnut patch. The first winter male northern parula since 1992 when one landed on the garrison. Obviously picked up on the storm with all the red-eyed vireos. Probably perish in the Atlantic...." His knowledge was boundless. What kind of man was this? The ultimate male chauvinist. A hopeless anorak? Maybe both?

"You know you're obsessive when other birders think you're mad," he volunteered with surprising candour. "It's above everything else in my life. My first thought when I wake up in the morning is: "What birds are going to show today?"

This 34-year-old ex-DJ from Little Chalfont, Buckinghamshire proceeded to unburden himself in the most remarkable fashion. This was the story so far: he'd begun by collecting dead birds from the roadside at the age of eight. Now he'd ticked more than 5,000 species in various corners of the UK. After a mind-numbing spell in the design shop at Vauxhall Motors, when he tried to sublimate his natural instincts, he saw a half-open door and bolted.

Paradoxically, freedom itself turned out to be a trap: "It got worse and worse. Like being on drugs. If I tried *not* to go for a bird I knew was out there, I got dreadful withdrawal symptoms. Pacing up and down the room getting edgy, unable to eat. Now I realise I've got to get in my car even if it's a yellowy browed warbler I've seen 500 times before. There's no choice."

Speed is of the essence in Lee's world. Traffic cops all over the country have

I first met him on the Scilly Isles one October and was struck both by his profound knowledge and his haphazard grasp of reality.

felt the draught of his birdmobile. Some don't get that close. Notably on the A90 between Perth and Aberdeen one arctic February dawn in 1987. Lee was in a hurry to catch a glimpse of roosting capercaillies and failed to see a chasing police car because his rear screen was misted over. He didn't even notice the overhead helicopter which tried unsuccessfully to arrest his progress. It was only when a police roadblock appeared on the horizon that Lee took his foot off the accelerator. The Sierra Cosworth he was driving had covered 117 miles in 46 minutes at an average speed of 142mph. For breaking the British record, he was banned for 10 years. It was commuted to 18 months on appeal.

Fortunately, Lee is a trained mechanic. With an annual mileage of 90,000 and fuel bills approaching £6,000, it's helpful if you can do your own servicing. Since 1974 he has covered nearly 1.5 million miles of tarmac in search of the elusive "mega-tick" (notable rarity). How many sales executives can match that? He drives himself into the ground fully aware that there's only a 65 per cent chance of success. Neither is there the consolation of great cmaraderie. "I wouldn't recommend this life to anyone. The tension's like piano wire and the back-biting is unbelievable."

There has, naturally, been a price to pay. His marriage survived the wedding day disappearance but only lasted 18 months. He was comatose for three months after a head-on collision with a lorry and his nerves have frequently been shrapnelled. "I was at the Rutland Bird Fair when the pager said that a middle-spotted woodpecker had been seen in Kent. Because I couldn't go I got so stressed out I collapsed on the ground. You know you're in trouble when it's that bad. It'll kill me one day."

Even fellow twitchers think he's off his trolley. Lee Evans would run through a brick wall to catch sight of a rare species – and frequently has.

Perish the thought. If Lee were to depart this mortal coil, the birding phenomenon, which now keeps a hard core of 3,000 zealots glued to the grapevine, could disintegrate in a shower of tripods, motor drives and CB radios. He's *that* pivotal. While his priorities may sometimes be open to question, his faith is copper-bottomed and his fever contagious. George Reszeter, one of the UK's leading photo-birders, an equally committed but marginally more grounded colleague, said: "There are twitchers and twitchers and there is Lee Evans. Plenty don't like him, others think he's barking, but you have to admire him."

The Duke of Edinburgh is of similar persuasion. He was prompt with his order when Lee's voluminous book reached the shelves. "Rare Breeds in Britain 1800 to 1990" lists every species recorded since 1695 and took nine years to compile. Its 2,000 pages were cut to 800 because the author couldn't afford the cost of printing. Quite how Prince Philip came to hear about the tome is uncertain. What we do know is that Lee personally delivered a signed copy to Buckingham Palace. I'm waiting for the sequel. It would surely have been under way if climatic changes hadn't interrupted Lee during these fallow months when he normally migrates to his own winter quarters – the writing desk. He reckoned without the Baltic freeze-up that drove a Bonaparte's gull to Oxton Reservoir in Derbyshire while unsettling an Arctic redpoll or two. Lee was forced to put his day job on ice and kick-start the Cavalier. Carmel bit her bottom lip. "You can never plan your diary because birds don't have rules. They only seem to turn up when you're otherwise engaged." Or getting married.

How Did It Get That Name? NOBOTTLE

The vicar of Lady Diana's former parish, Great Brington in Northamptonshire is no different from the majority of rural clergymen these days. He has to live in a modern vicarage scarcely big enough to accommodate the parochial church council, and he ministers to six parishes as best he can. A common enough tale I guess, but at least there's one church he doesn't have to bother with. It stands in the village of Nobottle, although 'stands' is something of an exaggeration. There's the church, albeit a steeple – look inside and there are no people.

Attendances at St John's began to dwindle when they demolished it. You think, as you drive past, that it must be an optical illusion, but it isn't. St John's, Nobottle, consists only of a tower and spire.

There was a church here once upon a time, built by the fourth Earl Spencer in 1865 as a retreat for his wife. The remains are Grade II listed and fashioned in attractive ironstone. The body of the church fell into disuse before the Second World War, presumably through lack of interest. It was knocked down in 1947. The tower and spire survived, not for ecclesiastical reasons but because the Ministry of Defence wanted it as a marker for the RAF.

The churchyard has become a manger for cows, protected by an electrified fence The spire's a pigeon loft. The sign on the padlocked door is not quite what you'd expect of a place of worship: "Danger. No unauthorised entry." I had a feeling the man in the big farmhouse might know something about it and ventured up the lane to find out. Robert Spokes thought I was just another inquisitive passer-by. They get lots of them calling in on their way to and from Diana's grave at Althorp House. He tells them the story of how he was the last person to be christened at St John's. What he doesn't tell is even more interesting. He has the only key to the tower, which puts him ahead of the vicar.

As we walked over the fields to unlock this strange landmark, Robert told me how he lost a sheep one day before the place was sealed to the public. To his dismay he found the errant ewe peering down at him from an open trapdoor on the first floor. I was tempted to ask if it was a sacrificial lamb but the creature was eventually coaxed back down the narrow stone staircase to safety. It was the only flock they'd had in there for years!

So, the oddly-named parish of Nobottle has no church, no pub, no school, no shop. But astonishingly it DOES have a dairy. The Heart of the Country game of coincidences was again at play. It's called Nobottle Dairy and it's owned by Ann Worle. What's even more remark-able is that Nobottle Dairy prides itself on plastic containers. In other words, there are no bottles in Nobottle. Convincing people it isn't a wind up is a constant irritation to Mrs Worle, who's had couriers fail to deliver parcels because they don't believe the address.

The Naked Farmer

There are several ways to get out of farming – none of them easy. Some diversify into bed and breakfast while others create farm parks and farm trails.

Dave Bailey saw if differently. His answer to the deepening agricultural crisis was to take his clothes off. It was a risk, of course. He could have been done for indecent exposure or he could have caught a cold. Fortunately he chose to disrobe at a sculpture college in Stoke on Trent where his conduct was much appreciated.

Dave Bailey, you see, has become a nude model. It only pays £6 an hour for one day a week in the Life Class, but it's preferable to being on the dole. It also gives him time to pursue his other career – part time fireman in the Staffordshire village of Ipstones. It's a job that, paradoxically, requires him to wear more clothes than ever.

Modelling is a drastic compromise for someone who only ever wanted to be a farmer. Two years ago he was proud of his herd of 60 pedigree Herefords, which he kept on the Staffordshire moorlands. Alas, BSE regulations meant that some of his stock was destroyed. He had no choice but to sell the farm and reassess his life – a decision since forced on many farmers by Foot and Mouth. In a sense Dave was lucky to get out when he did.

"To keep still for so long takes a bit of doing, but they like curvaceous models so I can keep eating the cream cakes."

Not being an exhibitionist by nature, nor an art lover of note, he didn't rush headlong into the fleshpots of Stoke. By chance, he happened to know the sculptor tutor, Rosemary Barnet, who'd lived in the same Peak District village. And by chance she happened to mention that she was short of models.

Desperate times call for desperate measures.

"I jumped at the chance," said Dave. "Although it felt funny to begin with I soon got into my stride, so to speak. To stay still for so long takes a bit of doing, but luckily they like a curvaceous model, so I can keep eating the cream cakes."

I caught up with him at the sculpture class. Clutching a 2-bar electric heater he made his way to a stool in the middle of the room. All around were men and women, waiting to see what he had to offer. He climbed up and gave them his best pose. After a few tweaks from the teacher, everyone was satisfied with his position and work began. Clay was daubed and stroked onto metal wire frames, pencils scuffed over paper, plasticine squeezed into shape. Dave's black Labrador settled down at his feet and curled up in front of the fire. It was clear that life in the studio suited *him* much better than the moors.

Work progressed. Eyes flickered constantly over Dave's body, the artists' faces taut with concentration. After twenty long minutes he was allowed to move.

"It's a skill, posing like that," said the teacher. "Most people simply can't do it. We're so lucky to have found Dave. He's a natural."

How do his mates react? "I had to run the gauntlet of jokes but they accept it now," he says. Even though it's not on view, they know where his heart really is. They know how many farmers were born to be farmers and can't see beyond it. That's when the trouble can start.

And what of the future? Says Dave: "I'll still be a nude model and I'll still be a fireman. By choice I want to farm again. Whether or not I get the chance is beyond my control."

He keeps the last two Herefords in a friend's field just in case.

The 'El Cordobés' of Staffordshire. Desperate times call for desperate measures and Dave Bailey's down to his hat and wellies.

Round The Twist

There's something crooked about Cleobury Mortimer in Shropshire. It's not until you stand back that it becomes obvious. A mile out of town, looking across the barley fields, you can see what the casual visitor might never notice. The spire of St Mary the Virgin is well out of true.

On closer inspection the parish church fails spectacularly to come up to scratch. It was clearly not constructed in the Perpendicular Period. Come to think there's *nothing* straight about the place apart from the vicar. Even *he* has to confess: "It's a miracle the church is standing at all."

The casual visitor wouldn't even notice anything wrong with the parish church at Cleobury Mortimer. In fact the spire leans 20° out of true.

He should know that the Reverend Robert Horsfield is, nevertheless very proud of his crumbling edifice. You don't go to the lengths he has, battling his way through a minefield of European bureaucracy, unless you feel a special affection for the church and the town. Thanks to his persistence Cleobury Mortimer is now on the world map. It has been accepted as a full member of the 'Association des Clochers Torts d'Europe – The European Association of Twisted Spires – joining Chesterfield as England's only representatives. If it takes a bunch of cowboy builders to get you in the record books. So what?

Actually, it wasn't so much the original builders of St Mary's, as the subsequent repairmen who should be held responsible. Frankly, they bodged it every step of the way. The main reason for the large amount of lean is that the oak ring frame, which forms the base of the spire, was buried in masonry during repair work and allowed to rot. It was worse on the south and west side, where the frame got wettest. Not until 1993 did a team of crack repairmen come to the rescue.

> *"We could see the main buildings moving beneath us. When we got back to ground level after four hours in the spire we were like drunks in the street."*

They were inspired by John Wheatley, an architect from Shrewsbury, who set about fortifying the twisted spire which bends 20 degrees out of true. As you enter Cleobury from the direction of the new vicarage you get the best view.

John and his team faced a stiff challenge. They also had to re-cover the Spire in wooden shingles, a monster undertaking which won them the John Betjeman Award for 'exemplary repairs to churches and chapels in England and Wales.' The experience left John groggy. "It was extremely noisy inside the spire. Every piece of timber seemed to be groaning, which isn't surprising when you consider the spire was swaying more than a metre from the centre line. We could see the town's buildings moving beneath us. When we got down to ground level, we were like drunks in the street."

Not doubting his word, I dispatched my fearless cameraman, Jamie Knights, heavenwards with a small camcorder so that we could get some impression of what John had been describing. We tried to envisage what it was like among the cross-timbers inside the top of that non-vertical spire and decided I was glad I wasn't a cameraman.

We felt much more comfortable inside the body of the church, where the vicar pointed out more structural discrepancies. The splendid Norman Arch was buckling under the unequal weight of the spire; the transept in which we stood was moving inexorably outwards. Indeed the Reverend Horsfield had weathered

That was all the encouragement I needed. Making a note of the vicar's name from the church notice board opposite the house, I continued my journey home. A telephone call the following day added more weight to my investigations. The vicar's wife confirmed that the place *was* inhabited and even took the trouble to pass on my name and number to her mysterious neighbour. She said he was perfectly charming, if a little remote.

"Oh yes, I drink. I had a serious attempt to drink myself to death but I got bored. Now I restrict it to a litre of vodka a week."

An interesting dilemma. Did I make a journey to meet him and try to arrange a time to film or did I just turn up with a film crew knowing that the best time to catch eccentrics is when they're least expecting it? He could only say 'no, go away' but that would have meant the best part of £1,000 wasted on the hire of a two-man film crew. That is the choice we're often forced to make on wildlife shoots, too. Animals, like eccentrics, seldom appear when you want them to.

I decided to take the risk. It felt like one of those one-hit stories where you don't get a second chance. Luckily, I was right. I knocked on his door a week later, not at all sure what to expect. As it happened, Nicholas Parker-Jervis could not have been more welcoming if he'd tried. He came around the side of the house, a tall, slim, white-haired man in his late 50's, maybe early 60's, wearing a baggy fawn cardigan with gaping holes in the elbows. He wore NHS spectacles and obviously shaved in stages, judging from the outcrops of stubble around his jawline. Either that or his eyesight was failing. He spoke quickly and nervously as though trying to condense his life story into a couple of paragraphs. A torrent of random thoughts and haphazard information tumbled from his lips. I had to slow him down.

It was hard work getting to the bottom of this extraordinary story, which went something like this: Nicholas paid £30,000 for the mansion in the early 1970's when he was firmly established as a high-flying stockbroker. He told me with a twinkle in his eye that he was earning £25,000 a year at a time when the chairman of ICI commanded a mere £20,000. Nicholas laughed self-mockingly as if to say: "look at the two of us today!"

His wife and kids left him 18 years ago and, as far as I could gather, moved further down the street. Only the cats returned. He went on: "The first morning I woke up in the house alone, it gave me enormous pleasure. It was so wonderfully tranquil."

You could say that again. He began to show me around the ground floor. I

How not to do it. A 12-bed Elizabethan/Roman Palazzo-style mansion, left to rot on the High Street like an abandoned car.

guessed most things were exactly the same as they were when Mrs Parker-Jervis left, except with eighteen years of grime and dust. Frankly the place was not fit to live in. Bare floorboards except in the living room, which was covered with a carpet he said was from his grandmother-in-law's flat. It looked like it – almost threadbare with a barely discernable pattern beneath the rubbish and splintered glass. The marble fireplace was Roman Palazzo style but looked as though it hadn't been cleaned in living memory. The room smelled as if it had once been used as a public bar.

Nicholas took me down an oak-panelled corridor (the once-beautiful wood now splitting at the seams) towards his office. There were some dusty book shelves, a desk, a telephone and piles of notepaper. There was also a photograph of a younger woman in a frame on the mantelpiece. He kept saying something about a woman friend who came to see him but it didn't quite ring true. How could anyone important in his life allow him to live in this squalor?

Nicholas excused himself. He had to climb up the observation tower to adjust the weather vane, which had stopped turning in the wind. I wondered why he'd bother with such a relatively trivial task when the kitchen sink and the bath were so thick with grease that you couldn't see any porcelain.

I was eager to find out where and why it had all gone wrong for Nicholas. "I lost my nerve in the City," he confessed. "It happens sometimes but you never hear about it. Just couldn't take the pressure any more so I ran away." To what, I wondered? "To this," he said, waving his arm with its moth-eaten sleeve towards what must once have been a very grand and ornate staircase. "I retired quietly and have been retired ever since. What's wrong with that?"

I sidestepped the question. He went on: "I haven't cleaned the bath for five years and I'm short-sighted so I don't even see the cobwebs. Don't they say a woman's greatest gift is to be unable to see dust?" Without changing gear he launched into his next mini-soliloquy: "Getting divorced would be costly so I can't be bothered. I'm still friends with my dear wife. I've got three children but they don't come to see me if they can avoid it. The locals think I'm mad. I'll accept 'eccentric' and make no effort to pretend otherwise. The house is run-down because that's my nature."

Strangely, *he* didn't appear run-down. Neither was he in the least concerned about heating. "I've got this woolly my dear mother-in-law gave me the first Christmas I was married. I've also got a sweater I used as a schoolboy and a cardigan from my dead father. That's enough to keep me warm."

Nicholas Parker-Jervis used to earn more than the Chairman of ICI. He was a whiz-kid stockbroker until he lost his nerve. You'd never know, would you?

It was lunchtime. Nicholas invited me to join him but I'd lost my appetite. We went into the kitchen, again festooned with cobwebs and littered with backdated copies of the Financial Times (that was consistent). Peeling the lid from a tin of sardines, he outlined his eating habits. Breakfast and dinner were identical meals. They consisted of boiled cauliflower, three raw eggs mixed with oatmeal, a teaspoon of marmite and some chopped tomatoes. It never changed. Nor did lunch: two rounds of toast, one with cheese, the other with a mixture of sardines and baked beans. I can think of unhealthier regimes. We moved onto the subject of drink.

"Oh yes, drink. I had a serious attempt to drink myself to death but I got bored. Now I restrict myself to a litre a week." "A litre of what?" I asked him. "Vodka," he replied, tersely.

That was as much information as I could extract. The rest was a jumble of chaotic facts and opinions, typical, I imagine, of someone who doesn't often meet people and gets out of the habit of conversation. I must say that despite everything Nicholas was managing reasonably well by himself and didn't seem to be under any particular stress. Even so, I felt a strong inclination to help him make a better fist of his unenforced exile, while recognising that was probably the last thing he wanted.

As I left, he wished me well with these parting thoughts: "I don't get lonely and I don't do boredom. There isn't time. I used to worry about the future but not any longer because there's so much less of it."

Now that they've closed Fish Hill and replaced it with a bypass, the only way to get a panorama of this spectacular valley is from the top of Broadway's famous tower .

Each county has its own identity and its own 'feel'. Worcestershire here, and Herefordshire were once lumped together. What a foolish idea that was. They're chalk and cheese.

A Fragrant Obsession

The gentlefolk of Wem had grown accustomed to Barrie Eckford's crusade. He'd been searching for his roots for at least a decade when I met up with him in this old-fashioned border town north of Shrewsbury. It was a few days before the annual Eckford Sweet Pea Festival, which transforms Wem into a global showcase. The event is named after Barrie's great grandfather, Henry, who was responsible for bringing this delicate bloom to Britain in the 1800's. The connection between Wem and sweet peas is purely coincidental but it became Barrie's life mission.

So that's what it's all about. Barrie Eckford is intoxicated by sweet peas and the legend of his great grandfather who sold the perfume to colonial toffs.

He was fighting his way through the brambles of an overgrown cemetery, eager to show me the monolith of a tombstone dedicated to his legendary ancestor. I could tell from the satisfaction on Barrie's face that he felt at ease beside Henry's monument. And yet a pale shadow of anxiety scudded across his eyes. What was it?

"It's an obsession," he sighed. "I'm obsessed with sweet peas and obsessed with my great granddad."

Although he lived in the neighbouring county of Cheshire, Barrie spent more time in Wem. It had been like that since he first discovered the place in 1988. He explained: "My father used to tell me tales of Henry and one August day, returning home from North Wales, I decided it was time to visit this place called Wem. From that moment I've never looked back."

Nor indeed has Wem. The year 1988 happened to be the centenary of Henry Eckford's arrival in the town. At the age of 65, the charismatic plantsman, who learned his trade in Edinburgh and at the Earl of Radnor's estate at Coleshill in Warwickshire, made what was a bold move for someone who'd already reached retirement age. Having obtained the only five varieties of sweet pea in existence and begun a mammoth hybridising programme, Henry established the world's biggest seed factory at a Victorian townhouse in Wem.

In for a penny, in for a pound, as they say. The attraction was more than 4,000 hectares of nursery ground on the outskirts.

Over the next 15 years he ate, drank and slept sweet peas, raising 200 new strains which were exported all over the world. Queen Victoria was a regular customer. So was the richest man in Britain, the Duke of Westminster, who, according to the accounts I thumbed through, still owes Eckford's £16 2s 6d! Henry was eventually awarded the Victoria Medal of Honour (VMH), which is the highest honour the Royal Horticultural Society can bestow.

How modestly it had started. Folklore has it that when Henry set out as an apprentice gardener, his mother gave him a sixpence she'd bent in two directions (an old Scottish custom) to last until he could earn sixpence of his own. When he died the twisted coin was found still sewn into the lining of an old jacket. For a hundred years the legend of 'Mr Sweet Pea' was forgotten, until Barrie, and a local grower called John Good, revived it. "This great man gave a beautiful gift to the world. The least we could do was remember him," said Barrie.

John pointed to the explosion of purple, red, pink and white in his own nursery: "Look at that mass of colours and smell the perfume. What's more, they replenish themselves every day. We owe it all to Henry."

Each July, Wem is awash with this derivative of the humble vegetable, which comes out of a frozen packet more often than a pod these days. The street names are adorned with a sweet pea motif. Around 3,500 visitors arrive by coach and car for the weekend festival. There are dozens of classes, squeezed into the Town Hall. Some people are reduced to sleeping in their cars because there's no room

Wem has become synonymous with Sweet Peas. Each July it's gripped by flower power as the annual show attracts visitors from all over the UK.

at the inn. Wem wasn't designed to accommodate such a big influx of people. And all this for a flower. Is it worth a crusade?

Barrie thought for a moment before replying: "I think everyone needs colour in their lives. Everyone needs fragrance."

It should have put a smile on *Barrie's* face but he still seemed preoccupied as he strolled in the sunshine through the market square. The centenary celebrations of 1988 had launched him on a genealogical trail which took him to Scotland and Canada as he uncovered generations of Eckfords. There was even an Eckford ranch in Manitoba. Not only that. Barrie had now devoted all his spare time to cultivating sweet peas in an attempt to emulate his great grandfather and local nurserymen like John Good and the late David Morlais Jones, who together scooped most of the prizes.

> *His love of sweet peas*
> *His intuition and his skills*
> *Brought flowers of great beauty*
> *To Wem and the World*

However, they will never be able to reproduce Henry Eckford's sweet pea perfume, purchased by colonial toffs for their distant paramours. John Cobbold, the chairman of the Sweet Pea Society admitted: "We've been trying to find the formula for years. We could raise money to help the town and the society. Unfortunately the recipe died with him."

And so far, there's no sign of a yellow sweet pea. The challenge to produce it ranks almost, but not quite, alongside the infamous quest for a black tulip. Curious that the most common garden colour cannot be replicated in a sweet pea. As David Morlais Jones told me before he died: "It's all down to genetics. I don't understand why we can't do it and nor does anyone else. If I got yellow I'd be a millionaire."

Barrie proudly showed me the stained glass windows in the Baptist Church and the plaque which captured the spirit of his relative:

Henry Eckford, born 1823, died 1905

"His love of sweet peas
His intuition and his skills
Brought flowers of great beauty
To Wem and the World"

But what about Barrie? Had his obsession left him more at peace with the world? Had his painstaking research into the family tree helped him to find himself? Again he paused before answering: "Not really".

The Big Picture

So, you want to be a landscape artist? In that case you'll need all the gear – fork, spade, rake, lawnmower and blowtorch. Forget the art shop – it's a trip to the garden centre. Oh, you don't mean that kind of landscape artist? You mean someone who actually creates pictures on the landscape. Forgive me. I had grander designs. I was thinking of the fellow who chiselled the White Horse or the Long Man of Wilmington out of the chalk hills. They were real landscape artists, just like Simon English, who is the 21st century manifestation.

Simon has crazy ideas: "I suppose I look at the land the way a sculptor looks at a piece of wood or stone," he says. "He can see his image in the grain of the wood or the strata of the rock. I can see it in the lie of the land."

He's not joking. The fields are his canvas; fire and garden tools are his paint-brushes. What he produces would make Michelangelo wilt, as we discovered on two very ambitious projects we filmed for the programme. One was a meadow brown butterfly. The other was a reflection of Kenilworth Castle in a lake that didn't exist. Nor, for that matter, does the castle – well hardly. There were many times when Simon questioned his own sanity. Come to think, anguish was a vital component in each of these masochistic exercises. It was as if he needed a heavy course of self-flagellation to enable him to bring his art to life.

Let's deal with the meadow brown. It was August somewhere in Warwickshire when I first saw the artist at work. The fields were a sandy-yellow after harvest; the hedgerows were tired and dusty like ageing visitors who'd outstayed their welcome. Apart from that ugly plant, ragwort, so detested by the horsy fraternity because of its poisonous qualities, there wasn't a wild flower to be seen. That's August for you. It was fine for Simon.

If the connection between art and lawnmowers had never occurred to me before, it began to take shape now. Simon was fever-ishly mowing a grass meadow 'loaned' to him by a farming friend who lived in the big house behind the redwood trees. It was roughly the size of a football pitch. The grass was straw-coloured and tinder-dry. So much the better, it appeared.

I must tell you more about the artist. He won a first class honours degree in Fine Arts some years earlier and earned most of his income lecturing. He supplemented this with gardening. A mile or so from the art meadow was a sunken water garden he'd carved out of an old rubbish patch. The water cascaded over stones to the Avon Valley 50 feet below. That's not all. Dominating this rustic scene was Simon's folly.

I can only describe it as a love bunker, the sort Adolf Hitler and Eva Braun might have enjoyed when the Third Reich was collapsing. Simon had designed the airshaft of this underground chamber to catch the midday sun. It was here that his friend, the farmer, proposed to his bride-to-be as laser beams of sunlight danced on the engagement ring. If it had rained, the ceremony would have been ruined.

To complete my image of this landscape picture-maker, suffice to say he sported over-generous side-whiskers, which curled southwards (from beneath a Wurzel Gummidge hat) to join an Abraham Lincoln beard (no accompanying moustache). Watching this tall, lanky craftsman dash around with his push-mower I couldn't resist the thought that once the grass was shorn to the prescribed length, he would do well to redirect the mower towards his imagined jaw line.

But I digress. Simon consulted his engineering drawings of the butterfly, which might have been composed by a draughtsman. It was all degrees and angles and measurements, as though art came out of a geometry set. The insect's body, made of black plastic sheeting and assorted compost, measured 20 yards in length. The wingspan was a formidable 50 yards. Simon erased the surrounding grass to leave the butterfly's wings exposed as thick straw.

He was working up a lather in the steamy morning heat: "Every time I do this I wonder why I punish myself but I know I've got to do it. I always underestimate how much hard work and worry's involved in trying to meet a deadline."

With that, Simon brought on a wheelbarrow of lime and shook the white dust through a sieve to create the butterfly's eye in

You don't often see zebras in Warwickshire – not this size anyway. Another masterpiece by Simon English who has chosen the most difficult art form imaginable.

a gap in the plastic sheeting. He proclaimed: "In meadow brown language, that spot says: 'This is me!'"

I'd hired a light aeroplane in order to film the completed sculpture because the scale of it was too large to appreciate at ground level. But Simon hadn't finished yet. The difficult bit was still to come. The antennae. Hence the blowtorch. Alas, the grass was too dry and caught fire. Delicate lines were swelling into charred

"Every time I do this I wonder why I punish myself but I know I've got to do it. I always underestimate how much worry and hard work's involved."

corridors as a forest fire threatened to ruin three weeks' work which had cost him £500.

"Water!" he bellowed to his trusty sidekick, Nick, who had the unenviable task of running to and from the farmhouse with a single bucket as he attempted to douse the flames as well as Simon's mounting panic. "Quick!" he bellowed afresh.

Distraught and exhausted, the artist began stamping at the flames while his voice ricocheted around Warwickshire: "It's not going to work, Nick. I sacrificed a summer holiday with my children for this. Now the antennae are ragged and blurred. It looks more like a moth than a butterfly." The ultimate degradation if you're as precise about your work as Simon is.

He was too hard on himself. As we took to the air and circled the meadow the beauty of Simon's art was quite breathtaking. I marvelled that someone had the vision to sculpt something so perfect without ever having the opportunity to stand back and judge it. All that time and effort yet the butterfly would be swallowed up by the changing landscape within a few weeks.

"That's as it should be," said Simon. "To make something on that scale that has to be constantly mown and looked after would be pompous."

Kenilworth Castle was on an even bigger scale. When he began scorching the ground to carve a complex illusion, there was no sign that the great mere, which once carried boats to and from the castle, would reappear. It dried up in the nineteenth century. But there haven't been many summers and autumns as wet as the year 2000. To everyone's astonishment, Kenilworth Castle lake (one of Britain's largest inland water defences) made a comeback. It wrecked Simon's preparations. Fire almost thwarted him in the butterfly field — floods forced him to start again here. I can't think of any other artist who's at the mercy of the elements like Simon is. It's a tough vocation.

For my next trick, I shall create the reflection of a castle which barely exists, in a lake which certainly doesn't. You think I'm mad? Well, it helps.

Poor chap had to ditch the push-mower in favour of a hover mower, which he steered through the swamp like an airboat on the Florida Everglades. He was determined that the grass would be cut because once more a deadline beckoned. Simon had spent nights working out the mathematics of where a particular tower would have been reflected in the lake before the castle fell to pieces. Eventually he was able to draw a flat perspective of the reflection and, once the flood has subsided, peg out its shape with the help of a plumb line and a mirror. Then he burned the shape into the field. Was this art or science?

"Computers are wonderful calculators but they want you to tell them what to do. For that to happen I'd have to have all the information then pass it on. By that time the job would be finished." There's hope for the human brain yet.

Creating a reflection of what is no longer there, in a lake which doesn't exist, takes a special kind of talent. Simon has it, as thousands of visitors to Kenilworth saw for themselves. What they would never have guessed as they admired his masterpiece was the torment that lay behind it. This is how he rationalised his unique art:

"I'm serious about my work. I wouldn't risk my health and sacrifice my family time if I wasn't. I go from despair to elation and back to despair very quickly. Overcoming problems is a feature of my work. If there wasn't a risk I wouldn't be an artist."

The Man Who Changed Time

Time is a man-made device designed to prevent everything happening at once. The thought occurred to me when I dropped in at the neo-Georgian headquarters of the British Horological Institute, which 'hides' just off the A612 between Newark and Southwell. What on earth *is* the British Horological Institute and what is it doing in the Nottinghamshire village of Upton?

Anyone remotely interested in timepieces will know. Budding watchmakers from Ecuador to Egypt converge on this elegant stately home to perfect their craftsmanship and salivate over its unique collection of clocks. My visit was the start of an intriguing journey into the meaning of time.

I wanted to know more about William Willett, the wacky landowner who first advocated British Summertime and the battle he had to convince the doubters. The BHI curator interrupted his daily clock-winding routine to point me in the right direction.

At the other end of the journey was a lonely monument in a Kentish wood where, every March and October when we change the clocks, ramblers are

reminded of William Willett's crusade. I first saw the monument late one October when the sunlight was at its softest and the last of the summer flies were still hovering in the shade. Like many woodland walkers, I wondered why we should spoil it all by turning back the hour hand. Each year I raise the question but each year I fail to get an adequate response. I've learned not to ask the Home Office. They seem flummoxed by the question. The reason for plunging ourselves into mid-afternoon gloom eludes those whose job it is to enforce the return of Greenwich Mean Time.

"While daylight surrounds us cheerfulness reigns, anxieties press less heavily and courage is bred for the struggle of life."

The party line is that children in the north must go to school in daylight and farmers should milk, harrow and sow without submitting themselves to a furious diet of carrots. Both arguments are flawed. School children who leave home in daylight have to return in the dark and since milking parlours are lit and heated, darkness has little relevance. Nevertheless we must 'spring forward and fall back' with the clocks, whether we like it or not.

Imagine the task confronting William Willett as he tried to break through a wall of government incredulity with his Daylight Saving Bill at the beginning of the century.

"What do you mean tamper with Greenwich Mean Time? Have you gone stark staring mad?" GMT had been in existence for only 25 years and Parliament was over-protective.

If not exactly immortalised, Mr Willett, the master-builder from Chislehurst, is fondly remembered by walkers at nearby Petts Wood, who come to pay their respects at a stone obelisk erected in his honour – a tribute to "The Untiring Advocate of Summer Time."

Perhaps Lord Archer had something similar in mind when he proposed the abolition of GMT and an end to

While riding his horse on early summer mornings, William Willetts deplored the fact that farms and cottages had their shutters closed and no-one was enjoying the countryside with him.

THIS MAN 👉
INVENTED SUMMER TIME

William Willett, London builder who died in 1915, was ridiculed when he first suggested saving daylight by putting clocks forward an hour during summer. A year after his death the scheme was adopted as a wartime economy measure, and in 1925 an Act of Parliament made it permanent.

William Willetts, the man who invented Summertime, was dead before his idea got into the statute book.

those melancholy days of late November and December when it is dark by 3.30pm.

Alas, his fantasies went the same way as William Willet's Bill, even though most of the nation probably agrees that permanent summer-time would take some of the sting out of winter. But Mr Archer, and other light-minded souls, need not lose heart. "Mad Willett" finally won the day and the British Summertime Act was forced on to the statute book half-way through the First World War. Sadly, after a lifetime of campaigning, Willet died 14 months before this happened. At least he missed the public outcry. "We're on Prussian time – it's treason!" cried the antis.

Winston Churchill, then Home Secretary and a supporter of Willett, predicted in 1911 that a grateful nation would one day erect a statue to him and lay sunflowers at his feet on the longest day of the year. He was right about the statue. Local people also raised the money to buy the woodland and preserve it from developers.

It was in Petts Wood that Willett, while riding his horse early on summer mornings, noticed how many houses still had their shutters closed and deplored the blatant waste of daylight. My favourite passage from the campaign leaflets goes:

"Light is one of the greatest gifts of the Creator to man. While daylight surrounds us, cheerfulness reigns, anxieties press less heavily and courage is bred for the struggle of life."

Willett also declared that longer days would make more time for rifle practice for which "the nation may some day have cause to be thankful". Was he anticipating the Great War?

King Edward VII had heard enough. With glorious disdain, he declared Sandringham a daylight-saving zone and forged ahead with Willett's ideas, irrespective of Asquith's government. The King ordered the clocks to be brought forward an hour in May and instructed his staff to ignore GMT. Later he imposed the same rule on Windsor and Balmoral. Only a monarch could get away with it.

By this time, the electronic telegraph and the railways had prompted the need for standard time in Britain. Before that, each town kept its own time – and the difference between Kent and Cornwall was several minutes.

Railway timetables were becoming impossible, so Penzance and all points west were synchronised with London. Station clocks became as important as church clocks had been before people carried watches.

But even the most meticulous watchmaker in Geneva could not craft a precise timepiece because the earth spins around the sun in an elliptical, not circular, orbit. In other words, the sun travels across the sky at varying speeds throughout the year. That is why sundials are more accurate than clockwork. Indeed in February, the difference between the two is a full 16 minutes.

So, unless you feel sufficiently anarchistic to emulate King Edward, enjoy British Summertime while it lasts. And should you visit Petts Wood to admire William Willett's monument, take note of the inscription beneath the sundial:

Horas non numero nisi aestivas: I don't count hours – only summers.

He wasn't so mad, was he?

Railway timetables were impossible because each town kept it's own time. For instance, Lowestoft would be several minutes ahead of Penzance in the west.

John Merrick used to arrive at Long Buckby stationed in a separate coach and was driven to Byfield in a carriage with blackened windows.

Did the barman know anyone at the house? Was there a local historian in the area? He was sorry but he couldn't help. No matter – I was grateful for the tip-off. As I've said before, it's surprising how many stories and programme ideas are the consequence of casual conversations in the pub.

It didn't take me long to verify what the barman had said. A call to Northamptonshire Library Services and we were on our way. I confess I hadn't seen the film 'Elephant Man' but I ordered the book from my local bookshop (why use Amazon.com?) and within two days it arrived. The picture I was able to piece together was fascinating. Most people around the Byfield/Church Warden area weren't aware of their place in history, and of course at the time when the Elephant Man was in their midst towards the end of the nineteenth century, it was a closely guarded secret.

Redhill Wood, just off the A361 was, for three successive summers, the home of the most celebrated freak in British history. Unbeknown to all but a few landed gentry and their estate workers, the Elephant Man – real name John Merrick – had been granted a lifetime's wish to leave his London hospital and enjoy a few months in the countryside. His 'escape' was made possible by a well known actress of the day called Madge Kendall, who persuaded the Knightleys of Fawsley Hall at Badby to help a tragic 25-year-old hideously deformed by a disease we now know as neurofibromatosis.

At least, the actress considered him tragic. In fact John was an intelligent, artistic and well-read young man whose determination and self-esteem were still unscathed after years of appalling treatment. What was Madge's motivation? A touch of philanthropy no doubt, but Victorians were notorious for 'collecting' things and there's a good chance Miss Kendall was propelled by curiosity as much as anything else. Colin Eaton, the Chief County Librarian at the time, confirmed this theory: "It was the height of fashion for aristocrats. They wanted to be seen with a freak of nature. It was good PR."

What an unsavoury thought. In some ways Madge and her friends were no better than the folk who queued up to mock John when he was a reluctant circus act. Lady Knightly, a close colleague of Madge's, just happened to be a deeply religious do-gooder, who'd never actually met the Elephant Man but befriended him when he arrived at her Northamptonshire estate.

When he left Euston Station for his journey to Northamptonshire, John had a second-class coach all to himself. When it reached Long Buckby it was shunted into sidings to keep it out of the public gaze. Once the other passengers had

Redhill Wood, just off the A361 in Northamptonshire, was home to the
most celebrated freak in British History – yet hardly anyone knows.

dispersed, he was ushered out of the train and into a horse-drawn carriage with curtained windows to complete the journey to Redhill Wood. As those of you who've seen the movie will be aware, the Elephant Man was repulsive to look at. It required a major leap of faith to get beyond that first obstacle.

The plan went badly awry when John was escorted to a farmhouse on the Fawsley estate and introduced to a member of the staff who'd been asked to take care of him. The poor woman screamed, threw her apron over her head and ran off into the woods in floods of tears. It was a reaction John had grown accustomed to in his early days in the travelling circus. An unscrupulous showman had set up the Elephant Man as a sideshow – not uncommon in those days – and made a good living at his expense.

Joseph Merrick had the freedom of Northamptonshire and would wander the fields around Church Warden unseen and untroubled.

The showman treated John worse than an animal, thrashing him mercilessly under the merest pretext, until the authorities put a belated stop to it all. He was eventually cared for in the bowels of a London hospital under the supervision of the celebrated surgeon, Sir Frederick Treves.

For those three summers he was given the use of a gamekeeper's cottage on an adjoining estate to Fawsley and more or less left to his own devices. Occasionally the villages would catch a glimpse and some even stopped to pass the time of day with him. Fred Hutt recalls his father being a 'friend' of the Elephant Man:-

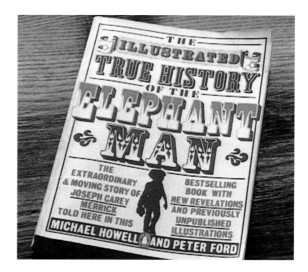

The book of the film – or should it be the other way around? At any rate it's a touching read.

"He often used to tell me about it. How intrigued the local people were by their summertime guest, and how surprised they were at his cultured voice. He couldn't pronounce the words properly because he was so deformed but he had a very gentlemanly way with him. He used to wear a broad-brimmed hat with a veil, rather like a beekeeper, so that people wouldn't be frightened."

Whatever the motives of Madge and Lady Knightley, the fact is that John loved to get into the countryside. As Sir Frederick wrote: "He'd never wandered among fields nor followed the windings of a wood. He'd never gathered flowers in a meadow. It was the supreme holiday of his life."

John Merrick wrote to Dr Treves about foxes and badgers he'd seen, daisies he'd picked, birds he'd heard and trout he'd watched darting through the River Cherwell. Simple pleasures, but what a relief for someone who'd spent his days entertaining voyeurs at the circus or hidden from view in a hospital basement.

In spite of the degeneration of his body, John remained good humoured until he died in his sleep in 1980 aged only 27. Although he was unable to smile or show any expression, he frequently told Dr Treves, "I'm happy every hour of the day." There's a lesson there somewhere.

The last place you'd expect to find the Café Philosophique.
How a rundown part of Derbyshire became a magnet for deep thinkers.

sell 'em cheap, he thought. Never mind that there was no passing trade. No matter if the likes of WH Smiths and Waterstones had already bagged all the trade there was. That was what he could afford, so that was where he would be. Somehow he would make it work.

David started going to salerooms, buying vast quantities of unsaleable books and stuffing them into what had been the living room. He dropped leaflets and notes through people's doors. He put up posters in town. He deliberately didn't keep any records of the titles he bought and refused to stick to a budget or financial plan. Where's the fun in that? The business didn't grow. It 'evolved'.

Looking at the shop now it's easy to see that David Mitchell's 'baby' has grown into an unruly adult. There are hundreds of thousands of books, some catalogued, some not, some in alphabetical order and others by subject matter. Books spill out from the original living room, up the stairs, over three upper floors and into the attic. One room is devoted to music, another to children's books. New books jostle with antiquarian. A wall of intense tomes on philosophy swings forward to reveal a café, hidden at the back. Through a heady fog of lentil bake and flapjacks people can be seen eating and reading their lunchtimes away, with the help of the gardening and cookery sections, both conveniently sited near the tables. Is this really Cromford?

"I am always finding books in the shop that I know nothing about."

It is a bookworm's heaven. Time stands still and waits for you to finish the final chapter. And there's always another room down the corridor where you can settle down and read. David doesn't know how many books he has. To him, stocktaking misses the point. The staff despairs. Their efforts to organise the chaos are met with non-co-operation. He's had to hand over the ordering of new books to a responsible friend who now runs the section with blistering efficiency.

Yet without David, Scarthin Books would be devoid of character. And it's character that has made the shop a success. His answer to the threat posed by internet giant Amazon was to open a site called www.bigsouthamerican river.com. Along with the more obviously-titled www.scarthinbooks.com it now accounts for a large percentage of sales.

"We could grow even bigger," says David. "We could move to larger, inexpensive premises in another location and start again, but to do so would mean becoming a seedling once more. And who knows what sort of tree we would grow into next time? We can only just cope with this business. We can't afford total chaos. The banks would foreclose on us!"

So instead of growing bigger, Scarthin Books has branched out sideways into another area – philosophy. Je pense, donc je suis, and all that stuff. Well, when you've read all there is to read in life, you have to share your wisdom. And so Café Philosophique was born – a club for well-read, lateral-thinking men and women searching for the opportunity to put the world to rights over a cup of Fair Trade coffee. After darkness, when the decent folk of Cromford are in bed, energy-saving lights glow from deep within Scarthin Books, while philosophers debate the meaning of Civilisation as we know it.

I joined them one evening. The proceedings began disconcertingly, with a can-crushing ceremony. Participants meaningfully squashed a coke can and placed in reverently in the recycling bin. There followed three rousing verses of an anti-pollution hymn before we settled down to the question of the evening, 'Ecology – science or religion?' Which turned out to mean, in layman's terms, "Is there any scientific reason for feeling so strongly about the environment or are we just a bunch of religious fanatics?" It was time to leave.

David started going to the salerooms where he bought vanloads of unsaleable books which he stuffed into his living room. If they were unsaleable, why buy them?

Sir Richard Arkwright's mill on the Derwent used to be Cromford's main landmark.
These days it's in danger of being upstaged.

High on the façade of the building stands a metal sculpture of the Goddess Amalthea holding the Horn of Plenty. The promotional leaflet says: "We have many of the best books on most worthwhile subjects and we constantly plug gaps. There is no space here to pile up bestsellers."

"I am always finding books in the shop that I know nothing about," says David. "And sometimes customers bring books to the desk with such arcane titles that I can't believe they come from our shelves. I almost think they *will* them into existence! My ideal customer is a passionate lay student, an amateur or even a professional who really wants to study a subject. We have the sort of books they'll want."

And if your search for that elusive title proves fruitless on all four floors, the leaflet has one final piece of advice. "Please ask where a book might be shelved before giving up hope!"

A few miles upriver Haddon Hall is possibly the best example in England of a medieval house.
Because it was abandoned for 100 years it escaped some of those awful Victorian add-ons.

Because of family connections, the slice of Derbyshire between Ashbourne and Bakewell (above) will always feel like a second home to me.

The Wrestling Baronet

Every village needs a Sir Thomas Parkyns, but only Bunny had one. At the time we were there to record the bizarre tale of the wrestling baronet, his former home, Bunny Hall, was a sad and derelict testament to a highly energetic man. There was rarely a dull moment in this small farming village south of Nottingham when he was in residence.

Sir Thomas was single-handedly responsible for reviving the ancient Roman sport of wrestling, which was on the decline in England by the early 1700's. Civilised folk had come to regard it as unrespectable – little better than street brawling. By 1712 you could be excused for thinking that Bunny was an ale-lout's paradise, because every man jack was pinning someone to the ground, including his lordship.

He'd pick impromptu contests with his coachman on the breakfast room floor and frequently embar-

rassed guests by launching into Greco-Roman manoeuvres at the most unsuitable moments. Shades of Inspector Clouseau and Cato.

The sport became so popular that Bunny staged its own all-England Championships. First prize was a laced hat; second prize was three shillings. I'm not sure what Big Daddy would have made of it.

Sir Thomas argued fervently that wrestling was indispensable to fencers and duellists, who could prepare for battle with less chance of killing each other – and published three editions of his manual called, rather oddly, "In Play" or "The Cornish Hug Wrestler".

Within those dusty tomes he wrote obsessively about the 'back clamp', the 'hanging tripper', the 'flying mare' and 'the buttock', moves of such esoteric grace that Sir Thomas was possibly the only person to fully appreciate them. Here's a sample from the second edition, which accompanied British troops to Italy during the eighteenth century.

Rather like Inspector Cluseau's sidekick, Cato, the wrestling baronet would launch himself at unsuspecting guests and pin them unceremoniously to the floor.

"If you have a contentious man that distrusts you and you would be ride of him, with your left hand take hold of his collar behind you and put your right hand between his legs as far as his codpiece. Then lift him up easily and thrust him out of the room."

Sir Thomas was a philanthropic squire and a great liberal thinker – but if he'd been a lollipop he'd have licked himself to death!

A useful tip at dinner parties.

It would be wrong, however, to assume that the wrestling baronet was a complete buffoon. His affliction was only partial. How do I know? Because his other great work of art was a sizeable treatise on manual labourers and how to get the best out of them.

Effectively, Sir Thomas Parkyns was a socialist peer. He became the first person to suggest and implement the minimum wage. His staff at Bunny Hall thought he was the bee's knees (when not called on to extricate themselves from a back-clamp.) Arthur Scargill would have loved him.

The reason I'm not entirely sold on the fellow is not simply that I dislike wrestling. It's more to do with his amour-propre. If he'd have been an ice-cream, the Lord of the Manor would have been in danger of licking himself to death. The evidence? How many people do you know, Jeffrey Archer aside, who would erect their own memorial in the parish church while they were still alive!?

Sir Thomas did, complete with a flowery epitaph in Latin and English, composed by none other than Sir Thomas himself. In case anyone in the village doubted his inflated opinion of himself, the wrestling baronet placed the said memorial at the altar end of the church so the congregation would have him permanently on their minds. I'm pleased to say that it caused a good deal of consternation among his adoring flock, who promptly shifted the statue et al to the back of the church once he'd breathed his last.

"If you have a contentious man, take hold of his collar behind you and put your hand between his legs as far as his codpiece."

That, however, was not before Sir Thomas gave them one last reminder of his eccentricity. Too old to wrestle or even hunt in his autumn years, he would climb to the top of the lookout tower at Bunny Hall, resplendent in hunting pink, to watch the hounds and hunters go by. He'd blow his horn and shout his hunting cries as though they could hear him. Sir Thomas cut a lonely figure by then. Lady Parkyns had long since flown the marital home to be with her lover in town. I wonder if she ever had to wrestle with her conscience?

What! No Poppadoms?

Curry restaurants have held a fascination for me since my sixth form friends and I discovered them in downtown Leicester. The city has become a spice Mecca now, but in the mid-60's there were only two curry outlets. If you could take a prawn vindaloo without smoke coming from your ears you were a man, my son. Our heads itched maddeningly; the sweat gathered around our temples; we hiccupped uncontrollably as those fiery chillies scorched our digestive tracts. The waiters chuckled at our stoical discomfort. *They* wouldn't have touched the stuff with a *garden* fork.

Such musings occupied my mind when I was filming an item about Midlands cuisine. I had lingered a-while in Chipping Camden, one of the livelier Cotswold towns, not quite so in love with itself as Broadway or Burford. I couldn't help noticing that Camden was a 'spice-free zone'. There wasn't an Indian restaurant

in sight. Could this be true, at a time when every English town boasted at least three, and even moderately-sized villages would have a takeaway if nothing else?

Not Chipping Camden. French, Italian, Greek, Chinese, yes – but not a chicken tikka masala to be had. There was a pub that organised the occasional curry night for those poor townsfolk who'd been denied the pleasures of the poppadom all these years, otherwise it meant a 10-mile round trip to Broadway. As we all know, Broadway is a divine but narcissistic community that normally can't bear to be tainted with the 21st century. Yet a curry emporium – an oversight by the normally omniscient Planning Department – had been allowed to appear at the far end of the High Street. It was very successful, of course. Chicken Tikka Masala after all is our national dish.

How and why had Camden escaped? I had a chat with Ana Choudhury, a friend of mine who ran the Prince of India chain through Buckinghamshire and South Oxfordshire. He was always on the lookout for new places to target. Although Gloucestershire was slightly out of his patch, Ana's eyes brightened when I told him about Chipping Camden. He'd heard of it but didn't realise it was as big as it was, and warmed to the prospect of breaking new frontiers. Why didn't we put our heads together and conjure up a joint venture? An interesting thought. A white man running a curry restaurant. Novel.

When I enquired further a stony silence fell over the town. Does Chipping Camden think there's something infra-dig about Indian Cuisine?

In the meantime, as they say, I conceived what I thought would be a witty programme idea. Why don't we examine the curry explosion through the English countryside and how it had introduced Asians to rural life when most of them would rather be in the city? Indian waiters, usually living in fairly cramped quarters above the 'shop' were the only non-Europeans you'd see in a village. A curious social phenomenon.

The idea moved to its logical conclusion. Why not arrange a 'curryfest' in Chipping Camden town square? Take the mountain to Mohammed. Mr Choudhury was happy to organise the food and the transport if I sorted out the rest. But would the council agree?" Town planners with a sense of humour are as rare as rocking horse manure (as Fred J. Taylor would say). This time I was lucky. The incumbent was on my wavelength. He saw the funny side. We could use an area of the car park next to the town hall one Thursday lunchtime. He even agreed to be interviewed about Camden's disinclination to encourage the opening of an Indian restaurant. This was precisely the kind of story that makes Heart of the Country different from 'worthy' competitors. While others lose themselves in

Indian waiters, usually living in cramped conditions above the restaurant, were the only black people you'd see in the countryside. A curious social phenomenon.

a miasma of environmental platitudes, I believe the best way to get across a serious point is to make it entertaining. Humour is a powerful conduit. Obviously there could have been racial undertones to this but, for whatever reason, you couldn't hide the fact that Chipping Camden had avoided any contact with India, Pakistan or Bangladesh. Snobs? The Town Clerk squirmed before confessing that I might have a point. Yes, there had been a few applications but they'd been turned down because they weren't considered 'right for the town.' Surely that smacked of snobbery? He didn't disagree. Other citizens took a more extreme view of the council's intransigence and welcomed us wholeheartedly – "about bloody time."

So we drove our sizzling roadshow into town one sweltering July day. Mr Choudhury and his team had done us proud with what was effectively a mini banquet. There were onion bhajis and portions of tandoori trout; there was chicken tikka, a lamb korma and king prawn bhuna with enough poppadoms and

What's that bread called, Nan?

naan breads to feed the entire county, plus dishes of lime pickle for those with a taste for danger. The curryfest was kept hot on an ornate trolley of burners, which created a unique spectacle in the town centre. As you can imagine, the aroma of meat and spices was intoxicating. Ana had alerted his Bangladeshi business colleagues who took the opportunity of promoting Lal Toffan, sub-continental lager brewed with rice. Chipping Camden's response was slow to begin with. I had visions of a communal snub. Maybe they were disinterested all along. However, word gradually got round that a free buffet and

iced beer was on offer during the lunchbreak. A chance for office workers and shopkeepers to find out what they'd been missing all these years. Hotel chambermaids abandoned their bedmaking to rubberneck out of first floor windows before being persuaded to join the party. It would be naïve of me to expect upwardly mobile elements of the population to be curry virgins, but some of the older generation certainly were. One old boy held his maiden poppadom as though it were a hand grenade and crunched it in his gums with the same degree of apprehension. A smile slowly crept across his sunburned Gloucestershire features accompanied by the memorable words: "Oi loikes these. What are they called? 'Pompadours' or summat?"

You can eat moussaka until it's coming out of your ears and stuff yourself with fish and chips until the cows come home. You can salivate over a lasagne or get to work on a crispy duck, but you *can't* get a chicken tikka masala to save your life.

An hour later we'd been well and truly swamped. The chicken tikka was first to go, followed by King Prawn Bhuna. The ice buckets for Lal Toffan were stuffed with empties. Operation Chipping Camden had been a roaring success and yet, to this day, unless I'm very much mistaken, there is still no Indian restaurant. I must have another word with Mr Choudhury.

The Quiet Woman

Let me tell you a tale about the quietest woman I ever met. She had precisely nothing to say for herself. A rare phenomenon and even rarer in the Derbyshire Peaks where countrywomen have been known to cut limestone with a lash of their tongues. Stay on the right side of them and you're ok. Step out of line and anything could happen.

So it was in the hilltop village of Earl Sterndale of the High Peak where men are men and women are content to let it be so. Except, that is, for one particularly long-suffering wife. Week after week she would turn a blind eye when her husband, a publican cum farmer, disappeared to Bakewell Market with his sheep and his drinking mates. It meant she had to run the pub on her own as well as looking after the livestock while he was away. Not to mention the kids and the housework.

Sensing there was no escape, he marched his beloved into the yard and removed her head with a meat cleaver.

Are you getting my drift? One Thursday in February he returned in a less-than active state. Not so much returned, as found himself deposited on his front doorstep in a comatose heap. It's remarkable what fifteen pints of Owd Rodger

can do to a chap. Barely compos mentis, he attempted, with only limited success, to effect a vertical posture before ringing the bell. It was nearly midnight. The regulars had long since gone home, their footprints now covered by fresh snow.

I dare say a good many readers will recognise the scenario — husband late home from the pub protesting his innocence and expecting to be treated like a wounded hero back from the trenches. His wife, for once, didn't see it that way, and it cost her the rest of her life. Fighting through layers of sleep, the dutiful spouse struggled downstairs to unlock the heavy oak door, which refused to swing open on account of seventeen stone of inebriated baggage emitting farmyard noises from both ends of its body. Welcome home darling!

Somehow she got him inside. A fatal mistake. He proferrered a few unfathomable excuses; she hit the roof. The tirade went on into the early hours, by which time the henpecked landlord began to recover his equilibrium. Sensing there was no escape, he marched his beloved into the yard and removed her head with a meat cleaver. The silence was golden. The blood and the body vanished under the snowstorm and stayed hidden until the murderer could construct his explanations which, as it turned out, required few frills. Villagers appeared to understand, if not exactly condone, his actions. In the interests of world peace he'd had to put an end to one of the most stentorian bouts of nagging ever to bedevil the hill community.

Villagers seemed to understand when the pub landlord put a brutal end to the most ear-splitting bout of wifely nagging to bedevil this peace-loving hill community.

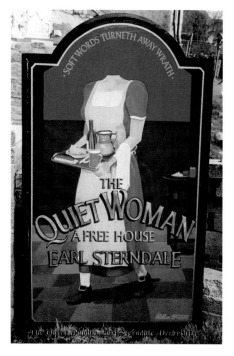

And that, readers, is why you will come across a pub in Earl Sterndale called The Quiet Woman and a sign depicting a headless form with the accompanying legend: 'Soft words turneth away wrath.' It is the only pub in Britain, nay the world, with such a name.

For the bare bones of this chilling tale, I'm indebted to Jenny Mellor, the current landlady. She did her best to keep her voice down during the telling of it, but couldn't avoid arousing her husband Ken, who'd just come in from feeding the pigs. I'm relieved to report that female emancipation has reached this altitude in the intervening years, so Ken was happy to corroborate his wife's story and add the piquant line: "The drunken publican had the sign put up because he wanted a quiet woman *outside* if he couldn't have one inside."

The documented history of Earl Sterndale is almost as captivating as its folklore. In January 1941 German planes were heading back to the fatherland over this part of Derbyshire and had a few incendiary bombs to offload

High among the crags of north Derbyshire I came across the quietest woman on earth. Barely a whisper tumbled from her lips. She'd learned a very hard lesson in this harshest of landscapes.

on the way. Checking their grid references, the pilots opted to drop the devices on Harpur Hill Munitions Store, but narrowly missed. One fell on the parish church of Earl Sterndale instead, the other on the Quiet Woman. Even in those days the congregation of the pub considerably outnumbered that of the church, so there were plenty of willing hands to douse the flames and save it from destruction.

Not so the House of God, which lost its roof, its east wing, the altar, the pulpit, the bible and most of the furniture. Neither faith nor wedlock is easily put asunder, however. A wedding scheduled for the very next day went ahead al fresco as though nothing had happened. Northern grit, or what?

Ken and Jenny Mellor were attracted to the place because of the dramatic landscape with it toothlike edges – and, can you believe, the peace and quiet. "Buxton was too noisy," said Jenny, "and Ken had always vowed to take charge of The Quiet Woman if it ever became vacant." Like his legendary and murderous predecessor, Ken keeps sheep, geese and an interesting herd of pigs, which prosper on a diet of leftover chips and beer dregs. Owd Rodger, of course. The customers benefit too because Ken sells his home-cured bacon over the counter. What goes around comes around.

And just in case you're wondering, Jenny *is* softly spoken. She also allows Ken a certain latitude, believing he would never abuse the privilege and roll up drunk from Bakewell Market expecting a hero's welcome. History is not on her side, though. What's more, Ken is a pipe-smoker and according to a police sergeant friend of his, pipe smokers rarely get into trouble with the law in Derbyshire. A curious observation, but apparently true. "You can't pick a pocket when you're lighting a pipe," says Ken.

There's a fair chance that if Jenny *were* to overstep the mark and lose her head as a consequence, Ken would simply light another bowl of St Bruno and deny all knowledge. He'd get away with it too!

Matlock And Chips

Blackpool without the beach.
Buxton without the style. That's Matlock Bath most Sundays in summer, when bikers clog the High Street and fish and chips clog the arteries. To see it at its tacky yet irresistible best you must go in August when the illuminations are on. I defy anyone not to be transported by this Monument to Bad Taste sheltering below the limestone cliffs off the High Peak. How green was the Derwent Valley. How multi-coloured it is now.

Matlock Bath is unashamedly downmarket, in stark contrast to the great spa days of the 1700's when the streets reverberated with carriages of the rich and famous and there was music and dancing every other night. Someone had discovered near-boiling water issuing from Masson Hill. Salts dissolved by warm underground streams seeping through the rock were deemed to have wonderful curative properties. The over-indulged came in droves, believing they could correct decades of bodily abuse with a few days in a bath.

The biggest limestone mine in Europe towers 100ft above your head in places. There's enough room here to build an underground city. Maybe someone will one day.

Eventually Matlock Bath was upstaged by rival hydros in Matlock proper so when the railway came to town in 1852, it re-invented itself as a working class playground. Over the Pennines came the cotton workers from Lancashire and the steelmen of Sheffield. Up the valley came the day trippers from Birmingham and Leicester. Matlock Bath was one of England's first inland resorts. Amusement arcades; paddleboats; Punch and Judy shows; fish and chip cafes. Nothing has changed.

On my last visit I counted no fewer than 27 fish and chip outlets along it's battered High Street, most of them serving mushy peas as well, which was okay by me. As evening fell, the illuminations combined with a thousand car headlights to create a surreal corridor of colours through the darkening hills. The smells were of vinegar, doughnuts, exhaust fumes; the sounds were of Britney Spears, Westlife, deep-frying fat and children's voices.

Daniel Defoe observed in 1780: "How different is the appearance of this place, once the habitat of grovers who dug for lead and lived in huts no bigger than hogsties." The ribbon of light looked even more surreal from a castle high on the hill where Andrew Pugh can enjoy the festivities without leaving his terrace. Andrew is the man behind the cable car ride that soars 450 feet above the valley and enables tourists to reach the Heights of Abraham without a twisting, stamina-sapping walk that used to be the only means of access.

The casual visitor probably takes the cable car for granted. He shouldn't. When it was installed in April 1984, it was the first Alpine-style cable car in the UK – a tribute to Andrew's perseverance in the face of local government, as well as geological handicaps. He overcame them all.

In fact Andrew made such a good fist of it that a similar system has been constructed on the Great Wall of China. Matlock Bath also gave him a ticket to Cape Town, where the South African government tapped into his expertise for a project on Table Mountain, and to London's South Bank, where he helped co-ordinate passenger capsules on the London Eye.

When they heard about the 400-foot cable car ride in Matlock Bath, the Chinese invited Andrew Pugh to advise them on a similar system for the Great Wall. Before long his expertise was in demand on Capetown's Table Mountain and on the London Eye.

And all of that from scratch. Andrew's knowledge of cable cars only began when his wife noticed an advert in the Daily Telegraph; 'Beauty spot for sale. Ancient caves and dramatic hillside.' The couple lived in Devon at the time. They'd never heard of the Heights of Abraham. They knew little about Matlock and precisely nothing about cable cars.

"We took one look at the place and fell for it," he says. That was the easy part. Their lives have been a challenge ever since. First in getting permission and raising £1 million to build the ride, then in stripping and restoring a former lead miners' pub 350 feet in the sky. In between the building had been converted into a pseudo-castle in typical Matlock Bath style.

It now sits immaculately refurbished like a peregrine falcon's nest on a ledge overlooking the River Derwent and the busy A6, whose roar becomes a whisper here among the clouds.

The town has another entrepreneur with equally eclectic leanings. Robert Aram collects disused cotton mills like you or I might collect Wedgewood pottery. I think he had five in his collection, but the trump card was Sir Richard Arkwright's water-powered Masson Mill, which dominates the skyline as you enter Matlock Bath from the Cromford direction. It was a snip at £245,000. Masson Mill is a throwback to the days when there were jobs in the countryside; when working-class people could afford to live in pretty villages and walked to work.

When the bell that called 500 men and women to work sounded for the last time in 1991, the mill had been in continuous production for 206 years. The Derwent Valley, like Ironbridge Gorge, was buzzing and smoking during the Industrial Revolution. So ugly it was beautiful.

So why did anyone want to be saddled with such a dinosaur today?

"Saddled? What do you mean, saddled? I regard it as a great privilege to own Masson Mill. We pass through history and forget it. Here's a chance to feel it and think about it." Robert's a fanatic in case you hadn't guessed.

He threw £4 million at it and 'hey presto' a rundown Victorian monolith became a shopping and eating complex and a living textile museum rolled into one. The looms still make aprons for visiting groups of schoolchildren. Some of the members of the old staff have been re-employed. One of them, Ian Page, told

> *The Derwent Valley was buzzing and smoking during the Industrial Revolution. Very Lowrie. Very lively. So ugly it was beautiful.*

me how he strolled past the old place many times wondering what would become of it, but never dreaming that one day he'd work there again.

Richard couldn't contain his enthusiasm. "Can't you feel the life of the factory again? Can you sense what a happy place it was?" I could, as it turned out. Good vibes. A happy and contented workforce? Apparently so. The only dispute lasted 90 minutes in 1923 when they put up the price of custard by a halfpenny. It caused a riot in the canteen. Temporarily.

One way and another, Matlock Bath has kept itself busy through the centuries, which is no mean feat for a country town. Lead mines, spa waters, cotton and now amusement arcades, flashing lights, fish and chips and cable cars. As long as Leicester, Derby, Sheffield and Nottingham evacuate their pleasure seekers and pack them off down the A6 each summer, it will continue to make a living. If, as hoped, they extend the railway line to Manchester it could transform the fortunes of this unique inland resort. Could the train help them to get back to the good old days of the 17 and 1800's, when 5,000 visitors a day would strain the foundations of the platform?

"It's wonderful to think that we might be inundated again," says Andrew Pugh, wistfully. "We have to concede, though, that the world has moved on since those times."

There Was A Crooked House

The Crooked House was a devil of a job to find and, once inside, a bit of a worry to negotiate. There wasn't a straight line or right angle anywhere. A couple of pints would've helped.

Searching for an unmarked farm track on a black August night in deepest Herefordshire was not my idea of fun. Especially after a long day and a three-hour drive. The clock in the car showed 9.35pm. The built-in mobile phone dial showed 'no signal'. Up ahead a 'T' sign along the rising country land showed that I'd reached the end of a long cul-de-sac. There was no room to turn around. What to do?

Those of you who have reversed downhill in complete darkness with six foot hedges pressing in on both sides will know how much there is to lose and how little to gain. The relief at eventually finding a wayside tavern in the middle of nowhere was instantly nullified by the landlord's blank expression when I asked about the Crooked House. He'd never heard of it. All was not lost however. Among the late drinkers was a foursome who luckily recognised my voice and, even more luckily, offered to lead me to the house in question.

That was my introduction to the most warped and twisted building I'd even seen. The couple who owned it were anything but. Marc and Tia Swan had created a home out of nothing at all. Not just a home, either, but a unique bed & breakfast establishment which attracted visitors from all over the world, despite, or maybe because of its very basic facilities. A small brochure warned what you *wouldn't* find at Crooked House – television, witches, junk food, central heating, children, the secret staircase and, last but not least, the fainthearted. I had an inkling of what was in store when I squeezed up a narrow, vertical wooden staircase to my room and slid between flannelette sheets into the four-poster featherbed. For now, sleep was the thing that interested me most. It came very easily.

Being an early riser, I was predisposed to a dawn call, which came in the form of a sharp sunbeam through the window behind my head and the shrill chatter of two-dozen swallows. I saw the room for the first time. The staircase was a dark well in a floor that sloped at least three different ways. The basin was an enamel bowl in a wooden frame, with a jug of cold water to one side. Shaving, shampooing and teeth cleaning was completed with some difficulty – the resulting bowl of soapy, whiskered water emptied into a bucket below the wooden stand, owing to the fact that there was no drainage. I discovered too late that there were baths by arrangement.

While Marc and Tia slept on, I went to explore. It was like being on board ship, a gentle swell constantly changing the horizon and making nonsense of conventional geometry. There was a window at 30 degrees to the ceiling line; a door which had more in common with a loft hatch because the principal movement was upwards rather than outwards, and a flagged floor with such a pronounced gradient you had to take a run at it to be sure of reaching the far end.

The lobby/breakfast room was the pick of the lot. Shafts of morning light edged their way through the front window to catch the magnificent cast iron range, hung with black pots and cauldrons. I opened the front door to get a proper look at the house, which I'd only observed from the inside. The sun was already warm. Droplets of water sat on the petals of Tia's wildflower garden, while an autumnal mist hung in the valley like dry ice. Swallows and sheep battled for audio supremacy.

By all that's logical it should have fallen down years ago. Thank goodness it didn't and let's be grateful for the courage and foresight of the owners.

The aroma of warm, wet vegetation accompanied me down the sloping path from the front door and across the grass to my car. The view when I turned around was such a kaleidoscope of colours, angles and perspectives that I needed a few moments to take it in. The business end of the Crooked House was painted red and could just about pass for normal. The rest could not. It was as though a gang of saboteurs had tossed away the spirit level and plumbline. Nothing was perpendicular or horizontal. The tin roof over the wooden half of the house sagged in the middle like a hammock.

"It's a house restored with love. That's what's missing in modern architecture. Everything looks the same. There's no feeling."

Disinfecting my shoes before stepping over the stile into the sheep pasture, I was eager to see the end elevation. This was the most bizarre aspect. The slate roof was bent like a broken leg and the window lines bore no relation to it. The combination of red plaster and pale blue woodwork stood out vividly against the green of the meadow and the wooded hills beyond. The chimney stack (almost vertical) was heavily clad in sempervivum, a climbing plant said to act as a lightning conductor.

Tia was up, admiring the swallows as they swooped over the corrugated tin roof and gathered on the telegraph wires next to Marc's workshop. Crooked House was his masterpiece. The shy 60-year-old, who rolled his own cigarettes and coughed his way through the first hour of the day, was a self-taught builder with a passion for the abnormal. The couple had come across this dilapidated sixteenth century farmhouse 20 years earlier, courtesy of a friend who owned a parcel of adjoining land. Whereas the majority of couples would have taken one look and politely back-pedalled, Marc and Tia were smitten. Said Marc: "I felt sorry for it. I wanted to do something to make it happy again, almost as if it was human."

Most couples would have taken one look at the decrepit farmhouse and fled. Marc and Tia Swan knew instantly it was for them.

Quite simply it was their dream home. Marc knew that the effect of two decades of weather on a building whose roof had blown away was not irreversible. This was a cruck framed house with a backbone of sturdy oak. The wood bent, curled and stretched but it wouldn't break. Tia was a former schoolteacher from County Durham who needed something different from life. She wanted to keep chickens, paint pictures, write stories and grow vegetables. The house came with a pigsty and several outbuildings. It sat on a hilltop surrounded by seven acres of land, one mile from the Welsh border. Perfect.

Restoration to Marc is different from what most people understand by the word. To him Crooked House would only by a worthwhile project if he could make a virtue of its imperfections. That's why window and door frames have never been allowed to assume a right angle.

That's why the roof is twisted like a necktie. That's why Marc built rooms into the roof space with bulging walls, dizzy beams and switchback floors. He explained: "It's a house restored with love. That's what's missing in modern architecture. Everything looks the same. There's no feeling. You can tell when you look at a new estate that the builders got no pleasure from building it."

Tia was making breakfast. Mushrooms sizzled in a pan on top of the range while bacon and sausages were hung on the metal hooks of what's called a 'hastener' before being turned to face the fierce heat of the grate. I don't need to tell you that the smell would have broken the resolve of the strongest vegetarian.

"In a few weeks my swallows will perform a fly-past as though saying goodbye and reminding their young where to return next spring. It's very moving."

My host had excelled herself, branching out into pub-sign painter, theatrical costumier, greetings card designer and manufacturer of leaded light windows. She also kept an illustrated log of the changing seasons along the lines of "Country Diary of an Edwardian Lady." It was full of stoats, foxes, grass snakes, badgers, hares and her favourite swallows. "In a few weeks from now," she sighed, "they'll perform several fly-pasts as though saying goodbye and reminding their young where to return next spring. It's very moving. Then they go to Africa and the skies are quiet."

There's a 20th-century kitchen where the couple keep a telephone in a wooden cabinet; a 19th-century kitchen and an 18th-century kitchen where Marc has created an 18th century glow by reducing the power supply to 12 volts, which lights small bulbs set in sockets along the beams. His great, great grandfather, Joseph Swan, invented the electric light bulb so Marc's resourcefulness should be no surprise. He also has a keen sense of mischief. The two-seater lavatory provokes unwelcome thoughts and there's a folly in the Pink Room, connected to the couple's bedroom by a hidden passage, which can only be negotiated sideways.

Marc tugs a length of rope and what seemed like a door leading nowhere opens into a wooden drawbridge, which descends gracefully to the vegetable garden below. The branch of an ash tree serves as the handrail. Under a large leaded window is an enormous structural crack that turns out to be one of Marc's little jokes. It was deliberately built in. We proceeded downstairs to the dairy, replete with vats of home-made wine, jams, chutneys, courgettes and tomatoes. The dairy leads to the larder and the most ingenious of Marc's inventions.

It might look like a scene from Country Living but don't be fooled. Nothing inside or out is quite what you think.

Instead of trekking to the hen house to collect her eggs, Tia has only to open a trapdoor in the larder and collect them from a straw-lined laying box. Yes, the hens come into the house to lay and a system of pulleys and strings allows a second trapdoor from the hen house to be closed remotely. All very well, but how do you get hens to co-operate? "It took two days to train them," said Tia. "I was amazed but it's true."

Having reached the top of the mountain, Marc has no intention of lingering to admire the view. His ambition is to build a crooked house from scratch. "It would make economic sense. Look at the Leaning Tower of Pisa. If they straightened it no-one would be interested." Faultless logic, so why not go ahead? "No-one's asked me and I don't have the money to do it myself. What I'd love to do is pre-assemble a crooked house and lower it by helicopter into the centre of Hereford. Then people would see that ramshackle is preferable to mass-produced boxes."

One day I'll go back to the world's most unusual bed & breakfast...if I can ever find it again.

Frozen In Time – A Miller's Tale

When the feeble October sun brings on the last of the apples you know it's cider time. Pippins, russets, jonagolds – any old garden windfall will do – claims John Stewart, who makes gallons of the stuff at Hoo Mill near Stratford-upon-Avon. When I dropped in he was struggling to find a bottle from last year's mix 'n' match crop to prove it. Unfortunately his friends had polished it off.

It's like that at Hoo Mill. John makes the cider and his friends drink it. Unsurprisingly, he has a lot of friends. The location helps, too. Lost in leafy Warwickshire, the River Alne's only working watermill stands in decaying splendour. Its mellow red bricks crumble into acres of orchards and fields. Heath-Robinson contraptions rust and moulder in the nettles. Sun-dried gates droop on broken hinges. In contrast the Alne divides neatly around and underneath the mill, driving the patched-up wheel with the force of a runaway freight train.

The skill is harnessing the power. It takes a lifetime to learn and makes you a slave to the river. Now turned 76, John is beginning to realise how much he has sacrificed to the mill: "I love it. It's my life. But I have to watch the water constantly. I don't know if I want to pass on such a burden to my family."

Living next to water always carries the risk of flooding, but an artificially created millrace demands never-ending vigilance. The heavy floodgates must be maintained and adjusted. When it rains, water levels need to be monitored almost hourly through the day and night. The bearings needs to be lubricated, the gearing greased. It's enough to make most people yearn for a hassle-free executive 'box' on a commuter town estate.

"It might have been different if I'd married," says John Stewart. "A wife could have smartened the place up a bit."

Hoo Mill is at a crossroads in time. Change it too much and you'd spoil it, leave it alone and you might lose it.

But not John Stewart. Quite the reverse. Not only does he welcome the extra work, he shuns all the modern conveniences that would make his life easier. Mains electricity? "Who needs it?" Drainage? "There's a perfectly good cess pit." Water? "I use spring water, and collect rainwater for my washing." Touché.

I followed him inside the mill house and groped for a light switch. A match flared and John lit the candelabra, gently hoisting it into place. "Tea?" he asked. He pumped a handle by the sink, filling the kettle with frothy water before

"They offered him a train ticket home to Stratford at Bow in East London, but there was a mix-up and he arrived at Stratford in Warwickshire! He had to find work pretty quickly so he asked for a job at the mill." The rest is history.

plonking it noisily on a decrepit Rayburn. "Fantastic, that Rayburn. Never let me down yet. My mother wouldn't have it at first. Too modern. She liked her range. But, within a week, you should have seen the cakes!"

John's mother would turn in her grave if she saw the state of her kitchen now. Thick grease from a thousand morning fry-ups seemed welded to the cream enamel stove and, try as they might, the dust-encrusted windows were unable to let in the light. Moving into the living-room I walked through festoons of cobwebs with the consistency of cloth. John looked uncomfortable. "Of course, it might have been different if I'd married. A wife could've smartened the place up a bit. I missed out there, didn't I?"

But it was a different story when John's great grandfather first bought Hoo Mill. In those days it was cutting edge – seriously hi-tech. Nineteenth-century millers were prosperous – the farmers dependent upon them to grind their corn. As we cleared some space and sat down on sticky chairs to drink our tea, John told me how his father fell on his feet when he wed the miller's daughter. It was a complete fluke. "He was wounded in the First World War. They offered him a train ticket home to Stratford at Bow in East London, but there was a mix-up and he arrived at Stratford in Warwickshire! He had to find work pretty quickly so he asked for a job at the mill." The rest is history.

John was born in the millhouse a few years later. His profound love of the place, with its family connections, has kept him tied to it ever since. His father had to accept that the mill could no longer pay for itself and rented the fields to caravanners in the '50's. From his tone of voice I got the impression that to John, this lack of sympathy with the character of the mill was sacrilege. When his

The reclaimed dynamo which is John's only source of electrical power. The rest is provided by nature.

father died, John dismissed the caravanners. The house, even then in desperate need of updating, became frozen in time. But the millwheel is all John requires in life. If he wants power, he simply harnesses up any number of machines to the wheel and lets it do the work. It runs the scratter for his cidermaking; it saws logs for the Rayburn. Thirty years ago he invested in a second-hand dynamo, which he attached to the millrace. He can charge batteries large enough to power a 40 watt light bulb and a tiny black and white telly. That's where hi-tech ends, however. The 'fridge' is a cold-slab, kept in the cellar.

A grandfather clock chimed the hour as I climbed unfeasibly steep stairs to view the bedrooms. John's — decorated in bachelor brown — looked as though a burglar with a vendetta had just left. Ivy had sneaked through a half-closed window and was growing across the ceiling. Only the bathroom had escaped the single-man syndrome. A pitcher and ewer sat on a pretty mahogany washstand and the walls were covered with decoupage, lovingly decorated, I guessed, by the Victorian lady of the house.

It was getting dark when John put the mill to bed. He turned a rusted handle and the wheel came to a smooth halt. "You can't have it going too much or it'll wear out." He adjusted the floodgates and checked the levels once more. That month the water had been dangerously high and he was careful not to slip. He'd lost his footing once and was flushed under the sluice gates — a terrifying ordeal that he didn't wish to repeat. "When there are floods," he sighed, "you wish you lived on a hill!"

He pottered back to the house, stopping to collect a couple of logs and some kindling on the way. He was expecting friends round that evening and was thinking of making one of his famous pump cakes. There's no shortage of company. Friends from those early caravanning years still come regularly to help him with the mill. Yet he worries about the future. He has no children. What will happen to his beloved Hoo Mill when he dies?

"I would like somebody to take it on and love it as I have," he says, "but it's asking rather a lot."

Canal bridges come in all shapes and sizes from old stone arches on the Worcester Canal to split bridges at Stratford – but it was bridges of a different type which inspired me to make a whole programme about them.

A Field By Any Other Name

Buttercups shone under a clear May sky, the creamy scent of early summer assailed the nostrils and somewhere in the middle distance, a cuckoo was doing its best to call a mate. The poor bird's vocal foreplay was half-drowned by another song, issuing from the meadow. It was choral, human and went like this:

> *"Far Field, Fallow Field; Far Field, Middle field;*
> *Far Field, Follow Field; High Hedges, Huckle's Hollow . . ."*

And so on.

I quickly realised that this was more serious than I thought. People don't stand in the middle of a buttercup meadow chanting madrigals for no reason. Peeping through the hawthorn hedge, heavy with mayflower, I had my worst fears confirmed. Was this was a breakaway group of 40-somethings tired of coffee mornings and Tai-Chi, who wanted to get out more?

The ringleader was a Pied Piper character who led the songsters from field to field enthusing about their ancient names as though she'd christened them herself.

We were in the partly-thatched Buckinghamshire village of Maids' Moreton. More on that in a while. The driving force was Paula Clair, a Pied Piper character, who led the songsters from field to field, enthusing about their ancient names. This is how she prefaced another round of agricultural hymn singing.

"Our poet imagined it was dawn, and the labourers were waking up to this wonderful song they'd heard from their ancestors."

And off they went into another stirring round of medieval field names, with Paula robustly conducting them. A passing farmer stopped his tractor, trying to make sense of this rural scene. To him, and the men from the Ministry, fields were just rectangles on a map with numbers. Paula's view was that their original names should not only be revived but turned into communal poetry. An old map from one of the Oxford Colleges helped them on their way.

"When we call a person by their name, we have a close relationship with them," Paula said. "So when we give a field a name we're opening up the oppor-

For the men from the Ministry, fields are rectangles on a map with numbers.
Paula, by contrast, knows their names and has a personal relationship with each meadow.

The Invisible Forest

How often do you see a farmer tending his fields with a JCB? Neville Bish did it all the time. He had no choice on one of the most peculiar arable fields you're likely to see. It was just outside Bourne, in Lincolnshire, where this long-suffering landowner waged a thankless war against an invisible enemy – the Iron Age forest, which lurks beneath his farm. You think I'm joking?

You might just have seen Neville kick start his old excavator on the stark, treeless acres which characterise this part of the country. The very idea of a forest on the edge of the Fens seems faintly ludicrous, but when the farmer anchors the JCB in the mud and smoke pours from a labouring engine which has bitten off more than it can chew, you know this is a serious business.

Half an hour passed before a gnarled, black tree trunk finally surrendered and was sucked out of the rich, peaty soil with its roots intact. What kind of place is this? Sweating profusely, Neville manoeuvred the tree to the edge of the field where, on closer inspection, I could see several more primeval shapes gathered like driftwood washed in by the tide. Yet we were at least 35 miles from the sea.

Of all things, the name of the bogwood furniture-maker is Peter Tree.

I'd been introduced to this lunar landscape by one of Britain's leading wood turners, who specialised in making Windsor chairs at the nearby village of Fulbeck. By one of those bizarre quirks, which happen a lot in Heart of the Country, the furniture maker's name was Peter Tree. It would be, wouldn't it?

Peter had first noticed outcrops of discarded oak and yew on his travels around this part of Lincolnshire. Intrigued, as you can imagine, he managed to locate the farmer who, far from being unco-operative, was mightily grateful for someone to take the offending articles off his hands. He had nothing but contempt for the stuff. When Neville bought the fields in the late 80's he had no idea he'd just become a subterranean forester. The farmer who sold him the acreage had never ploughed the soil deeply enough to know about these things. He might have charged extra otherwise!

Said Neville: "When I first started to plough and prepare the fields, I couldn't fathom why scores of timber outcrops kept appearing overnight. They wreaked havoc with my machinery."

The idea of a forest in the Lincolnshire Fens seems faintly ludicrous. That is until you plough the soil and it comes to the surface. Perfectly preserved timber which has been submerged for 10,000 years.

How Did It Get That Name? SNAILBEACH

It's 50 miles from the coast and there's no sand. Snailbeach is one of a series of exotically-christened villages which seem to litter the Shropshire landscape. Why Shropshire I've no idea, except that it's one of those counties where sheep outnumber men (or DID before the Foot and Mouth crisis) and grass still grows in the middle of the road. None of which helps us explain the ridiculous name, Snailbeach. So, let's split it in half and have a stab.

The 'beach' almost certainly comes from the Saxon 'batch' meaning a small group of houses. Hence Perkins Beach – a nearby village inhabited entirely by Perkinses. The postman must have had fun. Snailbeach didn't remain a small cluster of houses for very long, however, largely on account of an ancient by-law which declared that a miner who could get smoke up a chimney would be allowed to build a house on the same spot. What happened in Snailbeach is that a group of leadminers in the 1850's got together to erect a big chimney stack in double quick time, started a fire and were permitted to build a group of houses around the base. That's why the village is higgledy-piggledy.

It all went horribly wrong in 1895 when Snailbeach hit the headlines. A rope snapped at the pithead one frosty morning and the cage crashed to the bottom of the shaft.

Before I attempt to explain the 'snail' part of the name, you should know that Snailbeach Mine was the richest lead mine in Europe at the time, raking in a fortune for the Marquis of Bath who owned the village and the mineral rights. It's a crying shame he didn't invest some of the profits in a few basic safety precautions, but I don't suppose any of them did in those days.

A thousand men worked in the mine. None of them lasted until retirement. One local resident, Emily Griffiths, said she never knew her two grandfathers. Both were miners and both were dead in their '40's. Lead, of course, is extremely poisonous, but if anyone had an inkling of that in the late 19th century, nobody let on.

The dress code was primitive. There were no helmets, so the men wore curly-brimmed trilbies, hardened with resin. A lump of clay was moulded onto the front and a tallow candle stuck on top. To protect their feet from material falling from the roof of the mine, the men bandaged their toes individually, the way boxers wrap their fingers before going into the ring.

It's said to be the origin of the expression 'toe-rag'. Not many people know that.

It all went horribly wrong in March 1895 when Snailbeach hit the national headlines. A rope snapped at the pithead one frosty morning and the cage crashed half a mile to the bottom of the shaft. Seven men were killed as the frame was reduced from seven feet to twelve inches high in a micro-second. You won't be surprised to hear there was no compensation. Said Emily: "The men developed a strange fatalism. They almost expected what was coming. Death seemed to be around every corner, so the fear of it diminished over a period of years."

All very revealing but what, you might ask, has all of this to do with snails? Well, strange as it seems, that part of the Snailbeach name does have some basis in fact. The village, as I discovered, is crawling with snails. No-one's sure where they came from but you can hardly put one foot in front of the other without a close encounter of the mollusc variety. According the Emily Griffiths, and her companion Elsie Rowson, snails were introduced by the Romans who were the first people to mine in the area, long before the Marquis of Bath acquired the land. Since escargots were known to be a part of the Roman diet, it's quite conceivable that the present crop is descended from the ones that got away. I can find no other explanation for this overabundance of snails. It's a shame no-one bothers to eat them any more.

Even today the secrecy which surrounded them still persists in Whiteway. They don't want anything to do with strangers.

distinguishes Whiteway from any other village. That, and a certain secrecy which forbids most of the population to discuss their way of life with outsiders – especially television reporters.

With a little gentle persuasion we did manage to break through the unofficial veil of silence. I interviewed Jean Cowd who admitted that she broke with tradition and got married in the conventional way. Indeed, she and her husband were about to celebrate their sapphire anniversary. Why did she do it? "Because I'm a Christian," she said.

And the chairman of the Colony Society, Joy Evans, also risked the disdain of her fellow colonists by opening up, albeit ever so slightly:- "I'm talking to you for one reason and one reason only – because I'm proud of what we've achieved."

"Better to talk about it than be secretive," I offered as a rationale. She paused:- "It's not a question of secrecy – it's about being allowed to be private. I realise I'm sticking my neck on the block, but I don't want people to think we're trying to hide something."

I thanked her for her co-operation and hoped it wouldn't land her in trouble. She smiled and shrugged her shoulders.

Glasnost had arrived in Gloucestershire.

Underneath The Arches

They span rivers, roads, railways and ravines. They've been lived on, fought over, jumped from and blown up but otherwise taken for granted. Bridges. There's something about them, isn't there? Perhaps it's the fact that they connect two entirely different worlds – one that goes underneath and the other which passes overhead. Take a narrowboat through Birmingham or London and you barely notice the traffic and bustle above you. Take a car through the centre of town and you have no awareness of the canal below.

It was while filming a group of fishermen hoping against hope to pluck salmon out of the Wye near Builth Wells that I caught sight of a small suspension bridge across the river. It had the elegance of the Golden Gate, if not quite the grandeur. I watched a car being driven gingerly across and, from 250 yards away heard the

In the meantime, Paul and Julie Batty have a nice little number in the Cotswold stone cottage which comes with the manager's job. Paul retired from a posting with the RAF in Cyprus, seeing Swinford Toll Bridge as an ideal way back into the UK. The couple's consolation is a lovely berth on the Thames and a

seemingly endless parade of wildlife including a family of swans which feed at their back door, a resident fox, two kestrels and a badger which got himself into a bit of a fix just the other week. He'd somehow manoeuvred along the balustrade and onto the parapet before realising he was out of his depth. Before the RSPCA could get there, our intrepid badger made an almighty leap for freedom, landed with a sickening thud on the riverbank but, miraculously, waddled off none the worse for his acrobatics.

Paul's chief lieutenant, Alan Bailey, was the happiest toll collector I think I've seen. He spends most of his time 'trapped' for hours in the tight little booth dealing with an endless stream of drivers, some of whom resent having to pay. He's been doing the job for 15 years. "I like meeting people," he offered as an explanation. Queues began to form in both directions. There was no time to continue the conversation.

Apparently the Earl of Abingdon used to perch on a nearby hilltop on summer days and spend the time eating sandwiches while watching the toll booth through his telescope. Peculiar pastime. He would return to the bridge in the evening to check the day's takings and frequently upbraid the collector for being somewhat economical with the total. Thankfully for Alan's sake, the new owner is less severe, though they do have to keep a lookout for rebellious drivers.

Anyone refusing to pay or proffering a £20 note with the "sorry, no change" line has his number plate recorded and reported to the police if it happens again. The trickiest customer was a Japanese driver, who insisted on claiming diplomatic immunity rather than pay his toll. And that was when it only cost 2p to get across. He got away with it but they're waiting for him!

LINCOLN HIGH BRIDGE

Spanning the junction of the River Witham and the Fosdyke Canal in Lincoln is a rare specimen. The wonderfully photogenic Lincoln High Bridge – the only remaining bridge in England with shops and offices built on it. During the Middle Ages it was normal to cover urban bridges with house and shops – the rents paid for the upkeep of the bridge. Slowly the practice died out, but what we have left

Lincoln High Bridge was at the industrial heart of the city where wool was carried from the Midlands to Flanders and fishermen from Boston sold their catch.

By the time the Civil War erupted, Swarkestone Bridge was still the only crossing point between Nottingham and Burton on Trent. Sir John Harpur of Swarkestone Hall fortified the bridge and his own home against the threat of the Parliamentarians and Sir John Gell of Derby. The battle on the bridge was short but bloody. Soldiers pitched into the water and drowned in their heavy armour.

A century later Bonnie Prince Charlie set off for London. He reached Derby on 4 December, 1745. Seventy Highland soldiers were sent to secure Swarkestone Bridge, and they reached it four hours before Government troops. The Scottish soldiers held the bridge for two days before retreating in the face of obvious defeat. A monument nearby states that Bonnie Prince Charlie never made it further south than Swarkestone Bridge. He turned back to face the bloody battle of Cullodon. Unsurprising then, to hear that it is haunted. The ghostly sound of horses hooves can sometimes be heard crossing the bridge. But whose horse is it?

Back in the bar of the Crewe and Harpur Arms, our 21st century Bellamont sisters were getting into their costumes for our reconstruction. The horses and riders were standing by in the fields. Ian, the electrician, was adjusting and readjusting the lights. Tom, the assistant cameraman, was taking a crash course in driving the cherry picker. Now it was time to re-enact the past. With a growing band of onlookers the girls acted out the scenes. The horses refused to enter the water time and time again, giving us wonderful shots as they pawed and stamped. Finally, at 11pm , the electrician turned the lights full on. Instantly, the bridge shone out for miles around — majestic, shrouded in the soft mist, and decidedly eerie.

It was only when we arrived home that we realised we'd completely forgotten to listen out for the ghost.

SEATON VIADUCT

What's outstanding about Seaton Viaduct as far as I'm concerned is that it manages to look so perfectly in place. Twenty million bricks and 82 arches across a glaciated valley in wide open countryside should have been a brutal aesthetic invasion, yet man has the infinite capacity to create monuments which not only blend in with the landscape but actually enhance it. Seaton Viaduct is a case in point. Gaze along its three-quarter mile span from the pub car park at Seaton and you'll know what I mean.

This is the longest railway viaduct in Britain, crossing the border between Northamptonshire and Rutland with a quiet swagger, as if to say: "Rather dishy, aren't I?" Until the infamous Dr Beeching decided that gridlock on the roads

would be a better idea and closed half the nation's railways, express locomotives used to thunder over here day and night between London and Glasgow. Country folk felt their pulses quicken. "A fantastic sight," said Seaton resident, John Mayfield. "A rake of coaches shining in the sunset as the loco whistled and eventually disappeared into the tunnel."

Bernard Pridmore was a signalman at the Harringworth end of the viaduct. "You could see the trains coming right across the valley with the smoke drifting off the viaduct. Thrilling." His signal box was carted off to a museum but it takes more than that to keep him away. The day I was there 500 steam enthusiasts on a 12-hour round trip from the south coast were expected to traverse the viaduct at around 3pm. Unfortunately they would miss the full impact of this Victorian masterpiece because the one place you're guaranteed not to see a viaduct is when you're travelling on top of it.

I asked Bernard if he would be watching the steam train cross the viaduct. "You try stopping me," he said, challengingly.

I met this 70-year-old trainspotter in the White Swan at Harringworth, the Northants village which claims the celebrated edifice as its own, since the arches more or less slice through people's back gardens. Villagers in Seaton won't hear of it. "It's always been known as Seaton Viaduct and it always will be," John Mayfield assured me.

Man sometimes has the uncanny knack of erecting monuments which not only blend in with the country-side, they actually enhance it.

A trifle extravagant, I thought, to suspend 300 feet of steel cables over the river when a couple of wooden planks would have done just as well.

reneguing on a deal to maintain the bridge, until they were forced to behave themselves. I love stories like that.

Bit by bit the picture emerged. Llanstephan was built by Lord Milford of Milford Hall in 1922 so that people on his estate could have access to towns and villages on the main trunk road. A trifle extravagant to suspend 300 feet of steel cables over the river for the sake of his own small flock, when a wooden plank would have got them across.

However, when Lord Milford died the bridge was bequeathed to the nation, so to speak. Powys County Council acquired it in 1947 for the princely sum of £1 on condition that they would look after it ad infinitum. That's where the arrangement broke down. I'm sad to say 'looking after' amounted to doing naff all for half a century then closing it to traffic because it had become unsafe.

Standing on the banks of the river directly underneath the bridge, and hearing the conversation–stopping rattle of woodwork as a Land Rover thundered its way across, made me wonder about its safety now. It certainly felt rickety underfoot – the planks moved – but the true test was to drive over, which I did. It was a tight squeeze and a bumpy ride but a terrific view from the middle as the picturesque Wye tumbled over the rocks.

I was happy to have both wing mirrors intact on reaching terra firma, from where I glanced sideways to see cables bouncing the whole length of the bridge. That of course is part of the principle of suspensionism. To my amazement, a small queue had begun to form at both ends. The Llanstephan rush hour. It created an interesting dilemma. Would travellers stick to the rules outlined on the metal plaque – only one car on the bridge at a time because of a 5-ton weight restriction, and speeds not to exceed 4 mph?

Powys County Council sat on its hands for 50 years, completely neglecting its promise to keep the bridge in good condition.

The answer was no. Two cars engaged the planks while the car ahead of them was only three quarters of the way across. One imbecile gunned his VW Polo between the handrails as though on the grid at Silverstone. There's always one.

To get back to the story — thanks to the insouciance of Powys County Council, the towers of Llanstephan Bridge and the cable anchorages began to corrode. That's when the protesters stepped in with a campaign they called 'A Bridge Too Near.' Nice sense of humour. It worked, too. Powys was more or less forced to spend £130,000 restoring the bridge to its proper state. I'm glad. It deserves all the attention it gets. Lord Milford would be delighted.

years they despaired and handed it over to a distant relative of the Boultons. When he died, he left the whole estate to his business partner – my father."

Johnston senior took a long dispassionate look at the estate and was able to see the wood for the trees. The sentimentality of 'noblesse oblige' was dispensed with in favour of a paternalistic but fundamentally business-style approach. His

first move was to sell some of the outlying cottages, providing instant cash with which to commence urgent repairs to the rest. Many of the farms were auctioned off and the estate became smaller and more manageable. Fresh faces moved in and an air of expectancy began to develop. Empty cottages were let with low rents to those with skills that would enhance the area – thatchers, builders, tree surgeons, game keepers.

Thirty years on, it's hard to imagine there was ever a problem. The primary school playground is heaving with children. There's a

Nick Johnston has had to be brutal. There's little room for sympathy when you're trying to balance people's futures.

cricket team and a youth football eleven. The air is thick with fresh cream paint on newly-replaced window frames.

With no 'big house' to impress tourists (the main house is rather ugly and considered 'architecturally unimportant'), the Post Office has become the natural focal point. Its flagged stone floors and distressed pine fittings are laden with Great Tew branded produce and home-baked croissants. It's a goldmine – thanks mostly to the young master, newly graduated from the London School of Economics, but he's not too proud to stand behind the counter if the staff can't make it.

Away with the old style and in with the new – that's the Johnston school of estate management. None of that stuffy superiority of the landed gentry. Hard work doesn't frighten them and they're not embarrassed to mention the word 'money'.

"It's the bottom line," preaches Nicholas. "For the first time in a century, Great Tew is financially viable."

Unsurprisingly, they've trodden on a few toes. One old lady stopped me in the street to say how hurt her family had been by the changes. They'd rented one of the farms for generations, she said, but when it had been put up for sale recently they couldn't afford to buy it. At one time her entire family had jobs on the estate. Now they could no longer live or work in Great Tew.

"It is sad," said Nicholas Johnston, "but the estate can no longer guarantee

a job for life for anyone. It has to be a question of balance, otherwise the whole thing will shut down."

Great Tew may still look like a sleepy farming village, but it's a façade. Twenty farms have been whittled down to three and they just about pay their way. It's the rental from several cottages let to 'outsiders' at commercial rents that brings in the most income. A World War II airstrip on the estate is still maintained and is leased out to flying clubs. Part of the woodland has been transformed into a rally course. Even the abandoned quarry is being surveyed to see if any quality brownstone can be excavated. Land that cannot pay its way has to go.

For optimistic young couples who've moved into the village, life in Great Tew is good. The 'outsiders' pay vast rents for the privilege of living in a manicured toy town. Those who work on the estate have their houses maintained with the proceeds. There's money in the kitty for a rainy day. For those who say it's not like it was, there are as many who say "thank god."

I followed him back into the 'shop' for want of a better word. A stool piled with copies of the Hereford Times, a dusty glass cabinet containing bars of Cadbury's Dairy Milk and behind the counter an eclectic collection of light bulbs, biros, soap and baked beans loosely stacked on the shelves. The whole time I was there I never saw anyone buy anything. They simply collected their weekly papers and lingered for a chat. West End garage was more than a pavement petrol station. It was a meeting place, a pulpit, an advice centre and a pillar box. Was it viable, though?

"In any case, if I stopped running the petrol station I'd be over there in the churchyard."

"It's tough going, but you meet some nice old people," said Headley. "In any case, if I stopped running the petrol station I'd be over there in the churchyard."

Adorning the outside wall of the shop was a large advert for Raleigh bicycles painted on a green tin sign and evoking memories of the 1950's when Headley used to sell four cycles a week. He also mended broken cars in the garage at the back AND once sold petrol in 20-gallon cans to pilots in the fields across the way.

These days we only use the village shop in times of crisis, yet we expect it to be stocked with all the things we need. Headley told me about the bitterly cold winter of 1982, when Turnastone was under four feet of snow and cut off from the main arteries to Ross and Hay. Villagers came sledging down the hills in Klondike fashion, sucked the shop dry of goods, but forgot about loyalty once the thaw set in.

Where were those villagers now when Headley needed them to save his business? A couple of dozen had signed the petition, for what it was worth but local government didn't have a *great* reputation for listening to country folk.

Despite that, the protesters won the day. West End Garage was given a reprieve, although forced to convert to unleaded petrol before it could look the future in squarely in the eye.

Five years on, I turned off the B4348 once more and pointed my car in the direction of the Black Mountains, wondering if I'd find Headley again. In the hope that he was still serving petrol over the pavement, I'd allowed my fuel gauge to run low. Sure enough, the 'open' sign was still there. Everything looked exactly as it had. There was even a light in the shop window. Tentatively I knocked on the door and gave it a gentle shove.

Headley's eyes nearly popped out of his head. A broad smile took control of his face as he informed me that the petrol station was still in business. I wasted no time in filling up. Back at the counter I added a bar of chocolate to the bill

How he managed to support a family by selling petrol and chocolate bars in a hamlet on the road to nowhere I shall never know.

which Headley totted up with a pencil on a dog-eared notepad. Funnily enough, the switch over to unleaded petrol had earned him more money. So was he coining it? Had the petitioners continued to support him after the reprieve?

"No, they only come in dribs and drabs. They prefer to fill up in town. I make enough, though."

By chance, I'd called on Headley's 85th birthday. It was much like any other – just him and his terrier dog keeping warm beside a glowing coal stove in a living room overflowing with family photographs.

"That's my wife," he said, pointing to a small, framed picture on the table in front of him. "She died in 1986 but I kiss her photograph every morning and I thank God in church every Sunday for delivering me from war."

With that, Headley headed kitchenwards to cook himself a birthday lunch of roast lamb and carrots. Marvelling at his endurance I drove back to civilisation, still trying to work out how he'd managed to eek out a living selling petrol and chocolate in a hamlet on the road to nowhere.

They Counted Them All Out

I spent the early part of Remembrance Day, 2001 in a charmed village. It looked no different from a hundred other Cotswold villages tucked around a bend and behind a hill in this seductive landscape. There wasn't a soul on the streets at 8am. Smoke rose from a couple of chimneys and geese paddled in the stream next to the ford but that was about it for Upper Slaughter.

Even the church was closed while they installed central heating. Come December they'd need it. The wind hits you like flint out here. A sign on the church notice board said: "Remembrance Day Service will be held at Lower Slaughter at 10.45 am."

The sister village, a mile and a half down the road, suffered heavily in the Great War. Very few places in Britain were left untouched. At 11 o'clock on the morning of November 11, 1918 when the howitzers were silenced across the battlefields of Flanders and The Somme, every country parish began to count the cost. Families that had lost sons, fathers or husbands

Lower Slaughter's only a mile or so away but it lost a lot of men in the war.

were left with an awful emptiness. Eventually war memorials were erected across the land and Poppy Day became an institution.

But not in Upper Slaughter. Forty-four men went to fight in the trenches and forty four returned safely home to Gloucestershire without so much as a wound.

The inappropriately named Upper Slaughter had come through the Great War unscathed. Only 38 villages in England were similarly charmed, most of them in the Midlands. The list is on the facing page

That list was compiled by the well-known Nottingham journalist and author Arthur Mee, who wrote a book called 'The Enchanted Land' in 1936. Mee and his outriders travelled the length and breadth of the country between the wars in order to record 'the atmosphere, surroundings and very furniture of England.' What painstaking research it must have been to come up with a statistic like that. The lucky 38 were given the title 'Thankful Villages'.

County	Village	No of men who left and returned
Lincolnshire	Bigby	10
	High Toynton	14
	Allington	Unknown
Leicestershire	Willesley	3
	Saxby	Unknown
Gloucestershire	Brierley	14
	Coln Rogers	25
	Little Sodbury	6
	Upper Slaughter	44
Nottinghamshire	Wigsley	7
	Wysall	17
	Mapledeck	2
	Cromwell	Unknown
Rutland	Teigh	11
Northants	Woodend	19

The villagers of Upper Slaughter must travel to Lower Slaughter if they want to see poppies.
There's no war memorial in Upper Slaughter.

Lower Slaughter's the prettier of the two. In summertime you can't move for painters along the river basnks.

That, however, is only part of the story. Since he died in 1943, Arthur Mee would have had no awareness of what was to follow. By 1945 the 38 'Thankful Villages' had been reduced to just three in which the men survived *both* wars without a single casualty. They counted them all out and they counted them all back – twice!

One of the thankful three was Upper Slaughter. Another was Allington, near Grantham in Lincolnshire. The third was Coyton in Yorkshire. An extraordinary fact with no plausible explanation.

You will search in vain for a war memorial in Upper Slaughter. There's nowhere to lay a poppy wreath if you wanted to. The village was unable to hold a proper Remembrance Day Service because there were no dead to remember. Those who wished to pay their respects to the soldiers, sailors and airmen who'd since died of natural causes, did so at Lower Slaughter where the union flag flapped in a feeble breeze

"I might not have come home on several occasions, but I never told anyone in Slaughter about the close shaves I had. I didn't even tell my wife!"

and a solitary wreath lay at the foot of the war memorial. The congregation included half a dozen worshippers from Upper Slaughter, but no war veterans. Leading Aircraftsman, Percy Howse was the only one still alive and, at the age of 95, he'd just moved to a nursing home at Bourton on the Water.

Like many servicemen from both campaigns, Percy felt pangs of guilt returning from a war in which so many died. Why should he and his village be spared the grief and torment being endured by millions throughout Britain? A question no-one has been able to answer.

November 11th, 2001 was the first time for several years that Armistice Day coincided with Remembrance Sunday. While the bell tolled at Lower Slaughter, a couple of dozen people also trooped to Holy Trinity Church, 130 miles east at the village of Allington in Lincolnshire to add their voices to the national day of tribute. Most of the worshippers were aware that Allington suffered no service deaths in the Great War, but few seemed to realise that it had an identical escape in the 1939-45 conflict and of course the monument often mistaken for a war memorial isn't a memorial at all – it's the market cross.

THE GREAT WAR
1914 – 1918

Inhabitants of Upper Slaughter who served in a theatre of war
Sapper F. ALDER R.E
Corporal F. BATEMAN 7th Bn Gloster Regt.
Private C. BEAMS 9th Bn Gloster Regt
Lieut Col E. P. BRASSEY D.S.O. R.F.C Coldstream Guards.
Gunner G. A. BURTONSHAW R.F.A
C.O.M.S. F. G. B. COLLETT 7th Bn Gloster Regt
Serjeant R. G. GRIFFIN Cameron Highlanders
Private A. E. GUY 12th Bn Gloster Regt
Leading Stoker F. HAZELL R.N
F. H. HAZELL R.F.A
. . . A.S.C

Forty four men left Upper Slaughter to fight in the trenches – and all 44 returned home with barely a scratch between them.

A handful of veterans still exist in Allington, though none attended the service. The two we spoke to had each seen very active service – Ronald Atkinson with the Royal Engineers dealing with land mines and bomb disposal, and Gordon Woods in the Pacific with the Royal Navy. He told me: "The only narrow escapes I had were ashore." His wife was standing a few paces away – he didn't want to say any more.

Back at his nursing home in Gloucestershire, Percy Howse was a little more talkative, despite his 95 years: "I might not have come home on several occasions, but I never told anyone in Slaughter about the close shaves I had. I didn't even tell my wife!" I tried to persuade him to tell me more about his time in Algeria and Tunisia but he wouldn't be drawn: "It's a secret that will die with me."

Two of Allington's survivors share reminiscences by the market cross, which is often mistaken for a war memorial.

Percy's name is etched along with that of 39 other servicemen on a board in Upper Slaughter village hall, which records their safe homecoming. Jasmine Cottage, the house in which he lived for 67 years stands next door bearing a 'For Sale' sign. Percy had only left it a few weeks earlier. At the back of the cottage a stone lintel still bears the burn marks of an unusual wartime incident which took place while Percy and the other servicemen were away on duty.

For some reason Upper Slaughter was subjected to an incendiary attack of February 4, 1944. Houses and barns were set alight; farm animals panicked and bolted; villagers were seized by blind terror. One of them, a Mrs Poppet, who lived a couple of doors away from Percy, barricaded herself in the house when an incendiary bomb landed on her roof. The Fire Brigade hammered on her front door but she refused to open it. She thought they were the enemy. "I b'ain't lettin' them there Germans in for no money!" she hollered, as neighbours tried to reason with her, before eventually coming to her senses as the house threatened to go up in smoke.

It may have been that the Luftwaffe mistook Upper Slaughter for Little Rissington airfield, about 5 miles away. Had it not been for the firemen that night, the returning heroes, alive and unhurt, might have had no village to come back to. What a cruel irony that would have been.

The heroes of Upper Slaughter would have no village to come back to if the Germans had had their way in February 1944.

My Dream Village

I must tell you about a place called Aldbury and how it became an obsession. In the late 70's we decided to uproot from Warwickshire and move closer to London when I became ITN Sports Correspondent. Around that time, there was a popular TV series called The Shillingbury Tales, featuring Robin Nedwell, Diane Keen and Jack Douglas – a forerunner of Darling Buds of May or a visual version of The Archers, if you like.

The rural life it portrayed was what we'd all like it to be – cows in the meadow, ducks on the pond, horses clomping past an eighteenth century pub where farmers drank ale in an inglenook while discussing the annual tug of war match. These days, the farmers would be out of business, the pond would be full of super-market trolleys and the cattle would have been slaughtered.

I discovered that Shillingbury was, in fact, Aldbury – a village at the foot of the hills on the Buckinghamshire/Hertfordshire border with good rail connections to London and Birmingham.

It seemed too good to be true – and it was. Driving round a hairpin bend through dense beech woods, I first caught sight of Aldbury four hundred feet below me, bathed in sunshine with the Vale of Aylesbury stretching away into the distance. First impressions can be deceptive but are normally reliable in my experience. At ground level, the village really did have an eighteenth century pub overlooking the duck pond. Black and white houses intermingled with red brick cottages. There was a school, a village store and a pretty Norman church, all framed by the magnificent Ashridge Forest, which soared above them. And yes, they did have an annual tug of war match.

That was it for me. There was nowhere else I wanted to live. For a city boy who grew up in the terraced streets of Leicester, the combination of real village life and easy access to the metropolis was a cocktail I couldn't resist.

Unfortunately, I wasn't the only one. Young executives would maim to get a place in the queue. Bijou residences were snapped up at inflated prices almost before they came onto the market. We tried everything but were knocked back time after time. We even considered a half-timbered cottage on Main Street, which would have struggled to accommodate a family half the size and, can you believe it, had a Baptist chapel in the front garden. The chapel was a wooden lean-to, which had been used for services for decades. Worshippers were perfectly within their rights to march through the garden gate whenever the spirit moved them and attack the Baptist hymn book with bulging lungs, even though the owners of the house were trying to have a lie-in ten feet from the piano. The fact that I had it on my list at all is testimony to my blinkered view of the place.

Nearly 25 years on I'm no nearer to finding my dream home in Aldbury, but I've learned to live with it. Not least because it's only five miles away and I can enjoy a drink at the Valiant Trooper or the Greyhound while pretending I'm a resident. Which all helps explain why my dream village has appeared twice in the Heart of the Country series over the years.

The first occasion concerned the aforementioned duck pond, which not long after I moved to the area, resembled a moon crater. The water evaporated one dry summer and failed to reappear the following spring. Ducks were history; tempers were fraying; the regular stream of visitors to this Chiltern honeypot was down to a trickle. What to do?

The trouble with a dream village like Aldbury is that everyone wants to live there – and there simply ain't enough room.

Punches were thrown before the endless saga of the Aldbury pond was resolved. Beneath the old bakehouse chimney, which you can see next to the church, is a bottomless well which eventually supplied all the water they needed.

The history of Aldbury pond revealed some juicy morsels. A freak thunder-storm in July, 1988 had the pond overflowing across the village green, flooding roads and cellars. Once the torrent had forced its way over the higher ground near the Post Office, it had a clear run past the garage down to the Trooper, with dire consequences. A parish councillor, deemed responsible for what might otherwise be passed off as an act of God, was knocked to the ground by a blow to the face as civil disobedience took The Great Pond Debate into uncharted waters. The picture-postcard billa-bong, where sheep and cattle used to slake their thirsts and countless tourists picnicked beside the ancient stocks, had become a major political issue.

Because of its photogenic properties, not to mention its proximity to London, Aldbury was the film directors' favourite.

Only five months before the flood, the council had splashed out an unprecedented £8000 on a plastic liner but still it leaked. Is it any surprise that our pugilist saw red? The chap on the receiving end of the blow was Mike Balcombe, who absent-mindedly stroked his nose as he told me of the confrontation:

"Scapegoats were needed and I guess that if there's a parish councillor around, he's a prime target. I wouldn't have minded so much if I hadn't been putting sandbags down and trying to help."

While ponds were drying up all over England, Aldbury's was rescued by a gift of nature on its doorstep. Sixty feet below a 1750's bakehouse in the garden of a nearby cottage was an endless supply of crystal clear water from one of several underground aquifers. The owner, Robert Burrow thought of bottling the nectar commercially but settled for watering his runner beans instead.

Thanking the Lord for their deliverance from this impasse, councillors simply threaded a pipe under the road from the well to the pond and turned on the tap. For ten years now the centre of the village has been an oasis of fertility once more. Reeds and water lillies prosper around the fringes of the pond; swallows skim the surface; the ducks returned in legions.

At long last, Aldbury Parish Council could get back to the more regular business of where to site lamp posts and what to do about the proliferation of horse manure. Or so they thought. A time bomb had been ticking for years. Let's call it the Shillingbury Factor. Because of its photogenic properties, not to mention its proximity to London, Aldbury was the film directors' favourite.

It had starred in more movies than Julia Roberts — and was in serious danger of over-exposure.

It took the parish council years to cotton on to the fact that Robert Burrow's well was only a few feet away.

It was good fun in the early days when Robert de Niro came to stay at Stocks or when Michael Winner popped into The Greyhound for a beer. It was good fun when coach loads came to spend their money in the village they'd seen on telly. Adlbury had an impressive pedigree: Pie in the Sky; Inspector Morse; Plotlands; Parting Shot; Midsomer Murders; Bliss. In the early 90's, Richard Gere and Sean Connery drifted through the woods on the set of First Knight. You couldn't move without tripping over camera cables or bumping into the catering truck.

Back in the 70's Betty Bate got a whacking £500 a day for allowing her house to be used on film. Everyone in a black and white house, it seemed, dipped their bread. The rate for film and TV extras tempted housewives away from their coffee mornings and kids out of school. A couple of decades on, Betty's enthusiasm had waned: "The simplest things have become difficult. You try to get to the railway station and the road's blocked because they're filming. When you get home you can't park for the trucks."

Michael Winner's film 'Parting Shots' finally pushed the residents of Aldbury over the escarpment. The self-adoring film director commandeered the pond and the village green, turning them into the back garden of a house. Janet Bridle, a young mother with attitude who lived in a cottage overlooking the pond, was fuming:

"Every time a film crew arrives it's a bad experience but this was the limit. For two weeks at a time we had to put up with noise from 6am to 2am the following morning. You couldn't go in and out of your house for complete idiots swanking around as though they were something special. The whole thing was a pain in the arse."

Stocks – the former home of the Playboy 'king' Victor Lowndes. It was a den of iniquity. It's now a golfing hotel.

The parish council made more than £4,000 from film producers who think Aldbury's the ideal location. It paid for a new tennis court.

Janet would be the first to admit that her bank account was marginally healthier as a result. The church and the village shop also benefited and the primary school pocketed £3,500 when Carlton Television hired the building for the filming of 'Bliss'. Quite a dilemma for the council. They had set a filming rate of £800 a day but could probably have doubled that – such was the demand. How many villages enjoy that kind of luxury? The parish accounts showed an annual income of £4,170 from film producers and television companies. It enabled them to build a tennis court and erect a metal seat around the tree.

However, there were restrictions imposed by national government on the amount of money a parish could spend on itself. It was no longer an advantage to have large amounts of loot in the kitty. So a decision had to be made – would Aldbury continue to kneel before the God of the Silver Screen or would it make a stand for anonymity? A public meeting urged the council to exercise restraint in the interests of social harmony, so seven elected members went into session for two hours before coming up with a charter. Only ten days filming would be permitted in any given year, with no more than five per quarter.

A victory for commonsense, I'd call it. The truth can be hurtful but the conclusion I've reached is that Aldbury is probably best appreciated from the outside looking in. The price of being a honeypot is bees. I know, because I am one. We swarm all over the place when the sun comes out and sometimes when it doesn't. If you live there, you're bound to get stung.

Whether you're spying on peregrine falcons or admiring the river Wye on a clear summer's day,
Symond's Yat never lets you down.

Ledbury has provided a rich vein of stories over the years.
From the privately-owned railway station to the brilliantly-organised poetry festival. Lovely town.